SEA OF JAPAN

HOKK

① 1
② 2

③ 3
④ 4
⑤ 5
⑥ 6
⑦ 7
⑨ 9
⑧ 8
⑩ 10
⑫ 12
⑪ 11
㉗ 27
⑬ 13
⑰ 17
⑭ 14
⑱ 18
⑲ 19
⑳ 20
㉑ 21
㉒ 22
㉓ 23
⑮ 15
⑯ 16
㉔ 24
㉕ 25
㉚ 30
㉜ 32
㉖ 26
㊶ 41
㉞ 34
㉝ 33
㉛ 31

HONSHU

N

OCEAN

Castles in Japan

Charles E. Tuttle Co. RUTLAND · VERMONT : TOKYO · JAPAN

Castles in Japan

by Morton S. Schmorleitz

REPRESENTATIVES

For Continental Europe:
BOXERBOOKS, INC., Zurich

For the British Isles:
PRENTICE-HALL INTERNATIONAL, INC., London

For Australasia:
PAUL FLESCH & CO., PTY. LTD., Melbourne

For Canada:
HURTIG PUBLISHERS, Edmonton

Published by the Charles E. Tuttle Company, Inc.
of Rutland, Vermont & Tokyo, Japan
with editorial offices at
Suido 1-chome, 2-6, Bunkyo-ku, Tokyo

Copyright in Japan, 1974
by Charles E. Tuttle Co., Inc.

Library of Congress Catalog Card No. 72-91553
International Standard Book No. 0-8048 1102-4

First printing, 1974

Printed in Japan

Table of Contents

List of Illustrations

Acknowledgments

Few works of this nature are prepared solely through the efforts of the author, for others make contributions that aid in a book's success. This manuscript is no exception, and it is here I wish to express my sincerest thanks to Professors John T. Kinkel and George H. Kakiuchi of the University of Washington for the helpful suggestions they have made. The major contributor, however, has been my wife, Kiku, who has given encouragement, endured many a trek up castle hills during the research stage, and served as my interpreter and translator.

Grateful appreciation is also extended to the following authors and publishers for permission to use material from their copyrighted works:

Michael Cooper, S. J. They Came To Japan: An Anthology of European Reports on Japan 1543–1640. *Originally published by the University of California Press; reprinted by permission of The Regents of the University of California.*

A. L. Sadler. The Maker of Modern Japan: The Life of Tokugawa Ieyasu. *Published by George Allen and Unwin.*

Masaru Sekino. *"The Castle and Japan." This Is Japan. Vol. 8, 1961. Asahi Shimbun.*

D. Guyver Britton. *"Kanazawa: Water, Trees, and Lordly Grace." This Is Japan. Vol. 14, 1967. Asahi Shimbun.*

Rowland Gould. *"Hagi: The Town That Time Forgot." This Is Japan. Vol. 14, 1967. Asahi Shimbun.*

Figures 2 and 31 are based, respectively, on similar plans from the following, for which I extend my thanks:

A. L. Sadler. A Short History of Japanese Architecture. *Published by Charles E. Tuttle Company, 1963.*
Transactions of the Asiatic Society of Japan. *Vol. 8, 1880.*

I

Early Fortifications

◈ Introduction

Whether traveling through the lush countryside or exploring the concrete cities of modern Japan, the visitor is almost certain to notice physical evidence of Japan's feudal past. Moats, walls, turrets, and tower keeps of an age that ended just over 100 years ago are all there, evoking an aura of their special history. To the casual visitor these structures are hardly more than curious relics of the past, but if one makes an effort to examine their history, he will find them to be more than a curiosity. The castles of Japan are an integral part of both feudal and modern Japanese history. During the 14th and 15th centuries the petty feudal barons built defensive castles to serve as or to protect their residences. These fortifications also became the seats of government for the domains over which the barons ruled, and they became the social centers for the areas as well. It was also during this period that domestic and foreign trade began to flourish, thus adding increased status to the castle town as an economic center.

As the 16th century opened, the struggle between the feudal barons intensified with each one attempting to spread his influence over a wider territory. During this struggle the castles assumed greater importance as more people moved to the castle towns. The result was that these economic centers became increasingly vital. About 1542 the first firearms were introduced to Japan by the Portuguese, an event that radically changed the course of warfare. Defenses were substantially reinforced to offset the new weapons, and those barons who were not fortunate enough to have acquired them were defeated. By the end of the century almost all of Japan had been brought under the unified control of Tokugawa Ieyasu, who was made *shogun* (military ruler of the country) in 1603. Ieyasu set up his seat of government at Edo (present-day Tokyo) and from there administered the country as one feudal fief. The *daimyo,* or lords of the various fiefs, generally ran their domains much as the shogun ran the country. Similarly, the provincial castle towns began to resemble Edo, to the point where street names were identical.

Under Tokugawa rule, each fief was allowed to have only one castle; so all subsidiary strongholds were torn down, and the samurai who had manned them were transferred to the remaining castle and its town. This shift in population attracted merchants and artisans, and it was not long before the castle town was the commercial center of the fief. The samurai, who had little to do because there were no longer battles to be fought, became administrators, and many took up scholarly pursuits while others interested themselves in the arts. Thus castle towns evolved into commercial and cultural centers.

When the feudal period ended in the mid-19th century, the importance of the castle town did not diminish. Many such towns continued to flourish as population centers, and today half of the 60 or so cities with populations over 100,000 are former castle towns. That these feudal towns continue to be important administrative centers is indicated by the fact that 34 of the 46 prefectural capitals were once castle towns.

But the importance of the castle in Japan does not end with its relationship to modern urbanization. The architectural style employed in castle construction is one of the forms that is most truly Japanese in that it was relatively little influenced by Chinese design. This architectural style is called Azuchi-Momoyama after the period of history in which it developed. The amazing fact about this period was its short duration, for it lasted only from 1568 to 1603.

◈ From Prehistoric Times to the 12th Century

The earliest record of a defensive stronghold is in the *Kojiki*,[1] which mentions "rice castles" that, according to legend, dated back to about 25 B.C. The exact method of construction is unknown, but the *Kojiki* says they were inflammable. Garbutt[2] suggests that these walls may have been similar to the walls of French cottages, which were made of clay mixed with straw and could be burned with reasonable ease. This type of fortification was used during the age of clans before the country was united under one government, continuing until about the middle of the 7th century with little modification.

That the Japanese of this day knew about more substantial forms of defense is quite certain. The Japanese had invaded Korea in the 6th century and found not only castles with moats and beacon towers but also walled cities. In 544 the Japanese built six fortresses in Korea with a garrison of 500 men each. But for all the observations made by these island invaders, they continued to construct rather modest fortifications at home. One reason for this may have been the Japanese preference for fighting man to man out in the open rather than from a fortified position.

In 644 the Soga Clan is reported to have built moated palaces for its protection.[3] These had palisades and armories by the gates that were well stocked with arrows. The gates were guarded by husky armed men, and each gate was furnished with a water supply and wooden hooks to be used in case of fire, probably to pull down burning parts of the structure. About this time, the emperor ordered arsenals to be built for storage of the implements of war in the various districts and provinces. Those who lived on the frontier—that is, northeastern Japan—were commanded to keep their arms but to come together for their mutual defense.

By the mid-7th century Japanese efforts to defeat Korea began to fail because the Chinese also had the same designs on that unfortunate peninsula. Eventually Japan was forced to change from an offensive to a defensive policy after its last effort at invasion in 622. Upon withdrawing, the Japanese brought with them a number of Koreans of various stations in life. Some of the immigrants were employed in designing and building defenses in Japan against possible invasion by the Chinese. These were erected on the islands of Iki and Tsushima in the Korean Straits, on the island of Kyushu, and on Shikoku at Yashima and Sanuki. The new forts were more like castles and more elaborate in design than those previously built, but masonry was not used in their construction even though the use of masonry was known to the Koreans and Japanese since it was being practiced in China at that time. These more extensive defenses were rectangular in shape, similar in design to a Roman camp. The fort was constructed by digging a moat and using the earth from the excavation to form an inner bank with fence-like palisades that had openings at the top for discharging arrows. A boarded structure was later added to give better protection from enemy arrows. Gates were placed on the sides of the fort, and some had platforms manned by men with bows.

As the population of Japan increased, the frontiers of the country were pushed north and east from the Kyoto area. This effort to open new land was obstructed by the Ainu, a race of people who had settled in the northern part of Japan centuries before.[4] By the 8th century, the Japanese had populated the area around present-day Sendai and Akita. The Ainu had made life difficult for these settlers because of their raids, and the central government at Nara set out to pacify them. By 720 a frontier post was established at Taga, near Sendai. This post eventually expanded into a fortress and stockade. Later, other such fortifications were established at Izawa (near Hiraizumi), Akita, and Yuri (south of Akita). Ramparts were built at Kuriyagawa near Morioka and at Nutari (Niigata). Other forms of defenses were also constructed at various places in the area. In 776 the fort at Taga was destroyed by the Ainu, and it was not until 790 that the Ainu were brought under control and only in the early 9th century that the raids completely stopped and the fortress at Akita was abandoned. Recently it has been unearthed.

At the close of the 8th century the capital of Japan was moved from Nara to Kyoto (then known as Heian-kyo). Kyoto was a semi-fortified city $2\frac{1}{2}$ miles east to west and $3\frac{1}{2}$ miles north to south, and was surrounded by a moat and palisades. The large palace compound within the city was enclosed by a wall measuring 1,280 by 1,530 yards. The homes of the court nobles and other aristocracy could very well have been surrounded by moats and walls, for Lady Murasaki mentions them in her *Tale of Genji,* which was written in the early 11th century.

Fortifications did not change appreciably from this period until about the middle of the 12th century. One reason for their failure to change was perhaps that the warriors of that period did not want to take the time to build extensive defenses. Garbutt[5] suggests that another reason for the reluctance to build massive, stone-faced structures was the frequent earthquakes, which made heavy structures impractical. Much of Japanese architecture of this period was of light construction because of this danger.

◀ From the 12th to the Mid-16th Century: The Rise of Feudalism and Castle Construction

By the 10th century, the power of the imperial court had started to decline, and many landholders began to develop the skill of arms in order to protect their holdings from intruders and from roving bands of raiders. These warrior clans eventually were called upon by the court to enforce the imperial will. They were rewarded for their efforts with appointments at court as imperial bodyguards and as retainers of the Fujiwara Clan, which constituted the real power in the country. (During this era defensive structures consisted primarily of earthworks and stockades.) The most prominent of the warrior clans were the Minamoto and the Taira, whose members were direct descendants of imperial princes. The Minamoto had their strength in the north and east and were the dominant military class at court. The Taira were not far behind in their influence and had their power base in the south and west and along the Inland Sea, where they had gained skill in maritime combat. They also had a better knowledge of politics than the Minamoto and used this knowledge to advantage.

The Taira overtook the Minamoto in influence by always supporting the court whenever there was a dispute between it and the Minamoto. During the Heiji Rebellion of 1159–60, the Minamoto supported a faction of the Fujiwara Clan in a plot to overthrow the imperial government. The Taira intervened on behalf of the court and won a complete victory over the rebels, thereby gaining great power and, before long, complete control of the country. As time went on, the Taira became arrogant and were despised and hated in court circles. The decade of 1175–85 saw great hardship in the country, and for this the Taira were blamed, even though much of the distress was caused by natural disasters. As a result, the power of the clan began to decline, and its enemies rallied around Minamoto Yoritomo, whose base of power was centered in eastern Japan. The struggle between the two clans started in 1180 and lasted for five years, ending in a naval victory for the Minamoto in the Kammon Straits (between the islands of Honshu and Kyushu).

Yoritomo set up a military government, or shogunate *(bakufu)*, at Kamakura. He was made shogun in 1192 and thereupon established a feudal system that was to last until the Meiji Restoration in 1868. When Yoritomo died in 1199 his son Yoriie took over several of his offices but was not made shogun until 1202. During this time Yoritomo's father-in-law, Hojo Tokimasa, took command of the shogunate, because Yoriie lacked the essential qualities of an effective shogun. Murdered in 1204 (by his grandfather, it is said), Yoriie was succeeded by his brother Sanetomo. Sanetomo was a minor, and a member of the Hojo family served as regent until Sanetomo was murdered in 1219. Because there were no members of Yoritomo's line left to become shogun, the Hojo Clan took control of the shogunate. Succeeding shoguns were strictly figureheads, many of them imperial princes. The shogun's regents, under the leadership of the Hojo, continued as the de facto rulers of the country, and the Hojo enjoyed their position for nearly a century.

In 1268, when the Hojo regents were at the apex of their power, an envoy from the Mongols landed in Japan and demanded that Japan submit to the Great Khan in Peking. The Japanese rejected the demand and began to prepare for an invasion they knew would come. It was not until November 1274, however, that the invasion took place. The first Japanese islands to fall were Tsushima and Iki, but the main body of enemy troops was put ashore at Hakata on Kyushu. The Japanese were at a disadvantage because they had not fought a battle in 50 years, while the Mongols were seasoned warriors. The invaders had superior weapons such as powerful crossbows and machines for throwing heavy and combustible missiles. They also had the advantage in the way they maneuvered their troops, working them in formations, while the Japanese attempted to fight in their typical man-to-man-combat style. The battle lasted for a day, and under the cover of darkness the Japanese retired to their earthworks to lick their wounds. Only a threatening storm forced the Mongols back to their ships and thence to Korea.

The Mongols again demanded that Japan submit under threat of invasion, and again the Japanese rejected the demand. The country was put on a war footing, troops were trained, a navy of small ships was formed, and defenses were built. The latter consisted mainly of earthworks, but at Hakata a 10-foot-high stone wall was constructed around a large portion of Hakata Bay to hinder the invaders and make it difficult for them to maneuver large bodies of men.[6] The second invasion came in June 1281, when a force of some 150,000 Chinese, Koreans, and Mongols descended on Kyushu. The defending forces managed to confine the invaders to a relative small area, while a fleet of small vessels disrupted enemy shipping by boarding ships and setting them afire. The fighting went on for some seven weeks until a typhoon entered the battle and caused great damage to the invading fleet, ending the threat. The Japanese referred to this intervention of the elements as a *kamikaze*, or divine wind, a concept that was to be revived some 660 years later as a means of saving the empire in another war—that is, through suicide missions by one-man, bomb-carrying planes.

After this second withdrawal, Japan remained in a state of readiness for nearly 20 years. This drained the shogunate's resources, and it was unable satisfactorily to reward the defenders of the nation. The situation was one of several that led to the Hojo downfall. Another reason was the rivalry in the warrior class—a rivalry that had existed long before the Mongol invasion but did not surface until the Hojo were too weak to prevent open hostilities between the various clans. A dispute over succession to the throne, however, precipitated a climax and finally caused the Hojo to fall. Their headquarters at Kamakura was overrun and burned in 1333, and the rest of their forces were soon destroyed. One of those who turned against them was Ashikaga Takauji, who soon became the most powerful figure in the country and was eventually made shogun. He set up his seat of government at Muromachi in Kyoto. The succession dispute abated for a while but flared again and resulted in the formation of two separate imperial courts, the Northern and the Southern, the former supported by Takauji and the latter by his enemies. This split brought on a civil war that was to last for nearly 50 years.

By this time fortifications had become more sophisticated than the earlier earthworks, palisades, and stockades. During the uprising that overthrew the Hojo, Kusunoki Masashige, a warrior serving the deposed Emperor Go-Daigo, hastily built a fortress called Akasaka on the slopes of Mount Kongo. A rectangular fortification 650 feet square, the structure had 33 simple wooden towers of several levels each. These were enclosed for protection, had loopholes for firing arrows, and were connected to palisades. Part of the defending force was assigned to man the towers, and the rest hid out in the mountains. When the enemy warriors attacked, attempting to rush the improvised fort, they were thrown back by deadly accurate fire from the towers. While they tried to regroup, the defenders hiding in the mountains fell upon them, causing further loss. The defenders arranged logs and stones that were rolled down on the enemy in subsequent attacks, and used boiling water and pitch to greet those who attempted to pull down the palisades. Akasaka was finally defeated by siege, but the defenders managed to escape under cover of darkness before their supplies ran out. Higher on the mountain, Masashige had a castle that was built in much the same manner but was stronger and better manned. This fortress withstood all assaults and held out until the Hojo were overthrown.

By the end of the 14th century the succession dispute had been settled with the joining of the two courts. The Ashikaga were now at the height of their power. Within 50 years, however, their control began to decline because of luxurious living and the delegation of a great deal of authority to subordinates. These men were constables appointed to keep order in the provinces and collect revenue for absentee landowners. The constables had immense power to carry out their duties, and they shortly began to exercise that power for self-benefit. They amassed great civil and military strength and began to take over revenue estates owned by court nobles, monasteries, large landholders, and even members of the imperial house. By the end of the 15th century there were some 20 of these great territorial lords, or daimyo. During this period many of the smaller landowners of warrior descent who worked the land knew loyalty to no great lord. They joined into leagues to protect themselves from the constables and sometimes used their power to increase their own landholdings. Some of these, too, eventually became strong enough to be classified as daimyo.

In the first half of the 15th century, hostilities between the more powerful military overlords simmered while the overlords themselves strengthened their defenses and at the same time built barrier gates for both revenue and control over elements entering and passing through their territory. Defenses of that day consisted of deep, wide ditches that were sometimes filled with water to form a moat. Beyond these were steep, high embankments and stone walls. The moat was bridged with huge timbers leading to heavy wooden doors in the walls, some of which were incased in iron. In the inner court were defensive towers, the residence of the lord of the territory, storage houses containing food and supplies, barracks, and stables.

Hostilities flared in 1467, when the Onin War started. It lasted ten years and spread throughout the provinces. By the time it ended, Kyoto was nearly destroyed, and the flames of war flared intermittently for over 100 years. These battles were a struggle for control of the shogun, and through him, control of the country. At the same time there were internal struggles within the organizations of the great lords, for their vassals continually plotted to usurp the lords' positions.

During this period, as already mentioned, the castle town began to assume importance as a political and economic center. Urbanization accelerated when many daimyo compelled their vassals to live in castle towns. Here they would be on hand in time of emergency, and plots against the daimyo could be controlled. This movement of warriors was the beginning of the separation of the military class from the farmer class and was to assume great importance in the future social structure of feudal Japan.

The territorial lords not only concentrated on the arts of war but also stressed the development of resources in their domains. In some locales mining increased the wealth of the fief, and in many areas industry developed. Constant preparation for war also stimulated better communications, and roads were built and maintained throughout the country.

As the struggle for dominance increased in tempo, the warlords found it advantageous to construct strongholds other than those used for their residences. The typical stronghold had a fortification nearby that was built in a strategic position on a mountaintop or a similar elevation. Such a fortification was usually constructed in a location surrounded by trees and huge stones to make the site as inaccessible as possible. Neither the residential nor the "last stand" mountain castle was designed as a defensive position but, rather, as a protected site from which the warriors could sally out and engage the enemy in the open. As the era of warring feudal barons continued, castles became stronger and more elaborate. The stone walls grew more formidable, the moats wider and deeper. At the same time, however, methods of attacking these defenses developed, and miners from the mining provinces doubled as sappers to undermine the fortifications.

Around 1542 there occurred an event that was to change the course of warfare in Japan and to some degree the history of the country. This was the arrival of Portuguese traders, who landed on the island of Tanegashima off the southern coast of Kyushu,[7] and who brought with them some matchlocks—weapons that caused immediate excitement among the Japanese. For years these weapons were known as "Tanegashima," and their introduction eventually changed the architectural design of castles in Japan.

II

Military History and Latter-Day Castles

◈ From 1550 to 1615

Japan had now entered a period of decentralized and ineffective leadership. The feudal barons governed their fiefs as small kingdoms, and although they were not necessarily interested in expanding their territories, there was rivalry among them. Many wanted to bring the country under unified rule, and each coveted imperial sanction to accomplish the task, thereby becoming the military ruler of the country. To receive imperial support, however, it was necessary to march on Kyoto with an army to make a show of force, and this was almost impossible because it meant crossing the domains of other barons who had the same design. In addition, to leave one's fief without adequate defensive forces was an open invitation to ambitious neighbors to invade the territory.

One baron finally marched to Kyoto and received the coveted sanction. He was Oda Nobunaga, a minor chieftain in Owari Province, not far from the capital, who eventually overcame his neighbors and took control of the province. His first major victory came in 1560, when the powerful baron Imagawa attempted to move a force of some 25,000 troops through Nobunaga's territory on his way to the capital. With 3,000 troops, Nobunaga surprised the larger force during a rainstorm and caused it to retreat in disorder. Among Imagawa's officers was one Matsudaira Ieyasu, who later joined Nobunaga and changed his surname to Tokugawa. By 1567 Nobunaga had gathered enough strength to make the successful march on Kyoto. There he received the congratulations of the emperor, set up Ashikaga Yoshiaki as the 15th (and last) Ashikaga shogun, and became himself deputy shogun. Nobunaga later found Yoshiaki to be insubordinate and had him deposed in 1573.[1] After receiving his appointment, Nobunaga set out to subdue the country with his army, among whom was a man of humble origin who had risen to high rank. He was Toyotomi Hideyoshi, who was shortly to become an important figure in unifying the country.

Nobunaga might be considered fortune's child, for, although he did suffer some setbacks, circumstances were on his side in his important undertakings. He was usually at the right place at the right time, and the turn of events favored him at crucial points. He quickly learned the art of using the musket, a weapon that he procured in adequate supply while many of his adversaries had been slow to adopt it, either because of difficulty in obtaining it or because they lacked foresight in realizing its potential. In one battle he set up a zigzag pattern of wooden palisades high enough to prevent a horse from jumping over. His opponent chose the traditional tactic employing cavalry, while Nobunaga used an army of foot soldiers armed with muskets. As each enemy wave attempted to storm the palisade, one third of the 3,000 musketeers fired their weapons while the others prepared their slow-loading firearms. This continuous fire handily won the battle.

Nobunaga's most formidable enemies were the warrior monks of the Ikko, or Single-minded, Buddhist sect. The monks' main stronghold was at Osaka in a fortlike temple located on an island in a river.[2] They had a large following throughout the country and strong concentrations in Kaga and Echizen Provinces. Because of their wide holdings they had great wealth and military strength. They also had the support of several powerful clans, including the Mori in the west. In 1576 and 1577 Nobunaga led a series of attacks against the sect's outposts. Finally, in 1580, with their defenses seriously weakened, the Ikko warriors surrendered, but only in response to an imperial appeal.

During a lull in his fight with the Ikko militants, Nobunaga started to build his castle at Azuchi. The structure was the prototype of future castle construction, designed to complement, and defend against, the firearms introduced by the Portuguese. As we shall see in a later chapter, Nobunaga used stone as a primary building material at Azuchi, and the castle was provided with towers from which gunfire could be directed. It was during the construction of the castle that Nobunaga planned the final defeat of the Ikko warrior-monks.

The Mori Clan was almost the only remaining enemy of great strength. A campaign began in 1575, but progressed little until 1580, when Nobunaga's lieutenant Toyotomi Hideyoshi moved decisively against the Mori. During the siege of Takamatsu Castle in Bitchu Province, the daimyo Mori sent in reinforcements—a development that prompted Hideyoshi to call upon Nobunaga for help. Nobunaga thereupon dispatched a large force of men and went to Kyoto to prepare to join the battle. While he was in the capital, however, one of his own generals, Akechi Mitsuhide, fell upon him and killed him. When the news reached Hideyoshi, he quickly came to terms with the Mori and hurried to the capital to confront Akechi. In the sharp battle that followed Akechi perished and his troops scattered.

Hideyoshi now held a favorable position to take control of the country and complete its unification. He called a council of the four ranking daimyo (excluding Ieyasu) to decide on questions of civil government under the new regime and to distribute Nobunaga's estate. But as Hideyoshi outlined his plans for complete unification, those on the council began to oppose him, and it was not long before their disagreement led to a decisive clash of arms. The most important of these clashes was at Shizugatake near the northern end of Lake Biwa in 1583. After his victory, Hideyoshi enjoyed an even stronger position than before, at least for the time being, without any serious enemies. In 1584 Ieyasu met him in two minor battles in Owari. One of these was at Komakiyama (see Inuyama Castle, p. 118) and the other was at Nagakute. Ieyasu gained the advantage in both of these skirmishes, but neither he nor Hideyoshi was foolish enough to press the issue into a major conflict. The two reached a mutual agreement in 1585.

Ieyasu did not participate in any of the battles involving unification except during the Kanto Campaign, as we shall presently see. He spent his energy and resources strengthening his own position and extending his influence in areas east of Owari.

Hideyoshi now concentrated on subjecting areas farther from the capital. His next move came in 1585, when he brought the island of Shikoku under his control without much trouble. Kyushu presented a somewhat more difficult problem, however. Shimazu of Satsuma, in the southern part of that island, was a powerful warrior, and when he was ordered to submit to Hideyoshi's authority, he flatly refused. In 1587 Hideyoshi gathered a force of 200,000 and descended on Kyushu. All daimyo of the island submitted except the Satsuma forces, who fought against the invaders until they reached near-defeat, whereupon Hideyoshi offered a generous settlement. The offer somewhat reduced their holdings, but it was accepted. The lands confiscated in the Kyushu Campaign were distributed among Hideyoshi's loyal generals, one of whom was Kato Kiyomasa, who later rendered valuable service in Korea and became a renowned castle builder.

There were now no serious obstacles to unification. The Hojo Clan of Odawara, who ruled the Kanto (the area east of the Hakone Barrier and including present-day Tokyo), had not submitted, it was true, but its threat was minimized because Ieyasu acted as a buffer. In 1589 the Hojo daimyo was ordered to submit, and Ieyasu made every attempt to get him to do so. When Hojo continued to refuse, Hideyoshi prepared to move against him. Since Ieyasu's holdings lay in the line of march, and since he had been relieved of the burden of supporting the Kyushu Campaign, he was called upon to bear a major part of the expense against the Hojo. The offensive army began to move toward Odawara in April 1590 and traveled not only by land but also by sea. Hideyoshi preferred to use strategy wherever possible instead of slaughterous frontal attacks. In the case of Odawara the plan was to lay siege to the Hojo strongholds and let hunger and thirst effect surrender. A long siege was anticipated, and the invading forces, therefore, set up elaborate facilities of all kinds to keep the troops content and out of trouble. The arrangements included entertainers and courtesans, and the whole affair took on the atmosphere of a carnival. Both the pressure of the siege and internal conspiracy forced the defenders to surrender in early August. (See Odawara Castle, p. 84.) During the siege, Hideyoshi offered Ieyasu the province of Izu and the eight provinces of the Kanto in exchange for his holdings west of the Hakone Barrier. Ieyasu accepted the offer and moved to Edo Castle on September 1, leaving Hideyoshi in complete control of the country except for a few northern provinces still under the rule of a dozen or so barons. The most powerful of these was Date, who submitted to Hideyoshi late in 1590. Shortly thereafter the others followed his example.

In 1583 Hideyoshi started construction of his castle at Osaka on the site of the old Ikko stronghold. A massive structure, it rivaled the largest fortifications found anywhere. Following its completion three years later, Hideyoshi ruled the country from within its walls. In about 1594 he built another castle at Momoyama in the Fushimi district of Kyoto, wherein he showed his love of splendor in the structure's construction and furnishing. Indeed, it is from its architectural style and décor that the period of Momoyama art is named. In much the same manner he had built a richly decorated mansion in Kyoto called Jurakudai, or Mansion of Pleasure, in 1587, portions of which were later used in the building of Fushimi Castle.

Soon after he came to power, Hideyoshi instituted policies that were designed to strengthen both his position and the feudal system. He ordered a reduction in the number of small castles to prevent them from becoming bases for the potentially troublesome rural gentry. In so doing he tried to leave only those castles that belonged to his trusted retainers. At the same time he compelled his generals to relinquish their lands and move to other parts of the country. The object was, of course, to separate them from their ancestral power bases, thereby reducing their strength and potential for rebelling.[3]

In 1583 a land survey was begun, a project that was not completed until about 1598. The survey determined the tenancy of agricultural land throughout the country and assessed its value in terms of yield, particularly of rice. It was on this basis that taxes were to be levied, a policy that continued throughout the feudal period. The main purpose of the survey was to make the farmer the permanent tenant of the land he tilled and to hold him solely responsible for payment of taxes.[4] Upon completion of the survey all transactions in land were figured in *koku,* the yield from land stated in terms of rice or its equivalent (one koku=approximately five bushels). In conjunction with the land survey, Hideyoshi ordered a "sword hunt" in 1588 to disarm the farmers and prevent peasant uprisings. It also served to distinguish the farmer from the samurai class and to strengthen the feudal system. Both the land survey and the sword hunt had the same goal: to make the farmer subservient to the military class.[5]

Hideyoshi's next move was made in an effort to fulfill a long-standing dream: to subdue China and bring it under his control. The first step was to take Korea and use it as a base for future operations. A 225,000-man army and a 9,000-man navy were mobilized and assembled in Kyushu, and in April 1592 the invasion got under way with landings at Pusan. By mid-June the Japanese had advanced to the capital city of Seoul and occupied it. After regrouping, part of the invasion force advanced as far as the Yalu River, while other contingents occupied the countryside. During the inital phase of the invasion the better-equipped and better-trained Korean navy failed to interfere because it received no orders to do so. Once the command was given, however, it played havoc with Japanese shipping. The Korean army, on the other hand, offered little resistance, but irregular forces of farmers made a determined defense in the form of guerrilla operations.

The king of Korea retreated to Manchuria and sent an appeal to China for assistance. With Chinese entry into the conflict, there was some fighting and a period of truce before the Japanese were driven back to Seoul. Here they held off the Chinese for a time, but it was obvious that they could not defend their position indefinitely because supplies and reinforcements failed to arrive. In May 1593 they reached an understanding with the Chinese and withdrew from the city. Negotiations between Japan and China began, but they broke down in December 1596. A new invasion was ordered in March 1597, but the Japanese commanders saw little chance for success. Their forebodings proved correct when the Chinese and Koreans combined forces and eventually forced the invaders to a beachhead around Pusan. After several months of sharp fighting, news of Hideyoshi's death (September 18, 1598) ended the conflict and Japanese forces withdrew.

Before Hideyoshi died, he formed a council of regents of the five most powerful barons in the country, including Tokugawa Ieyasu, Mori Terumoto, Maeda Toshiie, Ukida Hideie, and Uesugi Kagekatsu. The regency was sworn to preserve the power of the House of Toyotomi until Hideyoshi's infant son Hideyori came of age and could assume leadership of the clan. Five lesser barons were appointed to the position of commissioners charged to carry out the orders of the regency. Their numbers included one Ishida Mitsunari, a man of great ambition who soon became an annoyance to Ieyasu. Upon Hideyoshi's death, Ieyasu assumed the position of head regent, but it was not long before the regency began to fall apart because of conflict among its members. After the death of Maeda Toshiie, who tended to hold Ieyasu in check, Ieyasu became somewhat autocratic and made decisions without consulting other members of the council. Both the council members and the commissioners harbored suspicions of his intent regarding Hideyori. Seizing this opportunity to increase his power, Ishida Mitsunari began to gather support to overthrow Ieyasu in Hideyori's name.

At first there were minor skirmishes that included two attempts to assassinate Ieyasu. Then came the siege and destruction of Fushimi Castle. A showdown battle was now inevitable, and the opposing forces began to march. Ishida headed the Western Army, which was a loose-knit body led by generals who were not necessarily agreeable to the concept of a central commander. There were also traitors in their ranks who would, when the battle reached its height, come over to Ieyasu's side. The Eastern Army, led by Ieyasu, was a cohesive force of well-coordinated troops under a unified command. Both armies were about equal in numbers when they met at the village of Sekigahara on October 21, 1600. The heated battle began at eight in the morning, and by noon reached its height. About this time the traitors came over to Ieyasu, and by two in the afternoon the ranks of the

Western Army broke and scattered. Ishida escaped but was later captured and put to death. Shimazu of Satsuma fief (one of the more important generals on the Western side) fled to his domain in Kyushu.

Ieyasu was now all-powerful. Within a short time all of the daimyo who had opposed him at Sekigahara had submitted. That is not to say that he was completely free from opposition, for those who had lost at Sekigahara were still loyal to Hideyori. As Hideyori grew older, he naturally resented Ieyasu for the way he was treated. Although he was allowed to remain at Osaka, he was continually pressured by Ieyasu, who, by 1614, had decided to destroy the House of Toyotomi and remove it as a threat to his supremacy. Hideyori sensed that an attempt to do away with him was imminent, and he set out to gather support. Many *ronin* (masterless samurai) answered his call and poured into Osaka Castle, an act of hostility that was all Ieyasu needed to justify a move against him.

In December 1614, Ieyasu gathered together a large host and laid siege to the castle in what is known as the Winter Campaign. In less than a month the two sides came to terms in which Hideyori agreed to allow the outer defenses of the castle to be destroyed as a gesture of his good faith. The Tokugawa forces went a bit further, however, and also filled in the inner moat.

Soon after the besieging army left, Hideyori again began to gather troops at the castle. When he ignored Ieyasu's command to cease this activity, the Tokugawa forces again descended on Osaka. This was the opening of the Summer Campaign, which began in May 1615 and ended early in June when the besieging forces fought their way into the castle. Hideyori committed suicide, bringing an end to the Toyotomi Clan. The Tokugawa were now supreme. Ieyasu died about a year later, but he had laid a foundation that gave his descendants rule of Japan for over 250 years.

The period of history just discussed might be referred to as the golden age of castle building, starting with Nobunaga's Azuchi Castle, which was designed as a fortification to resist forces armed with the matchlock. Its high stone walls, deep wide moats, corner towers, and tall donjon were intended to cope with this new weapon. At the same time the castle's design enabled defenders to use firearms to best advantage. Next came Hideyoshi's castle at Osaka, even more formidable and impregnable. These two structures set the pattern for later castle construction.[6] Most castles and castle ruins extant today were built in the short three-decade period from 1580 to 1610, employing the architectural design of the Azuchi-Momoyama period. It was then that Kato built his fortress at Kumamoto with its high, imposing walls, Ikeda greatly improved and enlarged the small castle at Himeji, and Ieyasu took the small castle at Edo and developed it into one of the largest fortresses in the world.

Shortly after Sekigahara, Ieyasu called upon the *tozama* lords to contribute heavily to the building of Edo Castle. These lords were those who were not related to, or had no hereditary tie with, the Tokugawa family and had remained neutral during Sekigahara or submitted to Ieyasu thereafter.[7] In addition to Edo Castle, they were also compelled to build other castles including those of Nijo, Hikone, Nagoya, and Sumpu, and to enlarge and remodel still others. Most of these castles were located in strategic areas between Kyoto and Edo and were built on the pretext of providing for national defense. Most, however, were never used in the kind of warfare for which they were designed. The building program was undertaken to reduce the resources of the tozama daimyo, whom Ieyasu did not trust, and to keep them under control.

Policies were also laid down by the Tokugawa government to control the tozama daimyo in ways other than financial. Castles were not to be built, remodeled, or repaired without permission from the shogunate. Men of the samurai class were obligated to live in the castle town. This requirement, an extension of Hideyoshi's sword hunt, tended to strengthen the feudal system. Marriages between the daimyo families had to be approved by the shogunate to prevent hostile alliances from developing. Tokugawa vassals were placed in fiefs where they could observe the activities of their tozama neighbors and report any evidence of conspiracy to Edo. They were moved frequently to prevent them from becoming too well established and forming alliances.

The daimyo were permitted to govern their fiefs without much interference from Edo, but they were obliged to observe the regulations imposed by the shogunate. Although they were allowed this freedom, they were required to alternate residence between their fiefs and Edo. This policy, known as *sankin-kotai*, was designed to prevent them from conspiring against the Edo government. While they were away from Edo, they left their families there as hostages. The traveling to and from Edo was another form of control, for the daimyo were expected to travel with a huge retinue, thereby incurring expenses that sapped their resources.

◧ After 1615

Peace had settled over Japan, a condition the country had not experienced for nearly two centuries. Some castles towns began to grow to metropolis proportions, especially those of the larger fiefs and those located on strategic trade routes. Castle towns of the lesser fiefs, however, produced small revenue and could not support large populations. They generally had a population equal to about 10 percent of their yield (*i.e.*, a fief of 30,000 koku had a population of about 3,000). Furthermore, many of the smaller fiefs had been established primarily for defense and were not intended to be rich commercial centers. As a result, the economic growth of the country was restricted to the larger population centers and to those towns that produced desirable consumer goods such as china and lacquer ware. Even the smaller castle towns, however, were important collection and distribution centers of economic goods.

The castle town was also the cultural center of the fief. Cultural development was concentrated in the larger population centers, but traveling troops of entertainers brought plays and other art forms to provincial areas. It was through this kind of activity that the country was culturally tied together. Many of the samurai, having little to do, turned to scholarship and philosophy, and a number of schools of political thought developed, both in the large and small towns.

But first and foremost, the castle town was military headquarters for the daimyo, and it was from here he ruled his fief. He built his castle to be easily visable from the town and the surrounding area, a constant reminder to his subjects of his power and hold over them. Although the castle was designed for defense, it was accessible enough so that the townspeople could reach it when they came to conduct business at the governmental offices located on the grounds.

As the Tokugawa era progressed, life for the warrior class generally went from good, to fair, to bad. The samurai had become accustomed to high living but their stipends (in rice) bought less and less. The shogunate suffered a similar fate and often was not in a position to help out in time of natural disaster. The economic power of the warrior class eventually passed into the hands of the rice merchants at Osaka and Edo, and it was an unusual daimyo who was not indebted to them much of the time. The merchants flourished, and some became quite wealthy, thus shifting the wealth of the country from the top of the social scale to the bottom.[8]

In 1639 Japan closed its doors to all foreign intercourse except with the Chinese, Koreans, and Dutch. Although others occasionally extended feelers on trade relations with Japan, no serious attempts were made until the late 18th and early 19th centuries when the Russians achieved some minor breaches in the seclusion policy. The British also renewed their attempt to trade, and American whaling ships infrequently put men ashore in search of supplies or sought shelter during bad weather. These activities caused the shogunate to set up coastal defenses and issue orders to expel the barbarians. In 1844 the Dutch gave the shogunate an appraisal of world affairs and advised that Japan abandon its policy of seclusion and open its doors to foreign trade. It was pointed out that Great Britain had recently forced the opening of China and that the same fate could be expected for Japan if she continued to repel foreigners; the shogunate rejected the advice. A year later the American Commodore James Biddle sailed into Edo Bay seeking trade and fair treatment of shipwrecked sailors. His request was rejected and he left. Eight years later, in 1853, Commodore Matthew Perry arrived at Uraga Bay near Edo with his famous "black ships." Presenting the U.S. request for the opening of trade and for fair treatment of shipwrecked men,

Perry made no threat but implied one when he informed the shogunate that he expected a favorable reply upon his return the next year. In 1854 a treaty was concluded, and Townsend Harris was established as consul-general at Shimoda. After much effort he achieved an agreement on opening several ports for trade; similar privileges were granted to England, France, Russia, and Holland within a short time.

The weakness of the shogunate was now very apparent and invited action by the tozama daimyo, particularly those of the Choshu and Satsuma fiefs, who rose in open revolt against the Edo government in the name of the emperor. Before long other daimyo joined the movement, and in 1867 the last shogun resigned in favor of the emperor. A brief civil war raged primarily in the north (notably at Aizu-Wakamatsu and Hakodate), ending with the return of power to the emperor after a lapse of some 700 years. Moving from Kyoto to Edo, the emperor took over the shogun's castle and changed the city's name to Tokyo, the Eastern Capital.

During the Restoration years many of the lesser castles were allowed to fall into decay and ruin while others were demolished. Some were sold for as little as seventy-five dollars for firewood—one was spared because no one was willing to pay that much for it. A corner turret of Ueda Castle was sold for about three dollars. Those castles allowed to remain were stripped of their outer defenses, and even those under imperial protection did not escape. In many cases the outer defenses were reclaimed by the castle town, which removed the earthworks and filled in the moat. Some of the remaining castles were used to garrison troops while others were made into public parks. Those under the protection of the Imperial Household were kept in reasonably good repair, but others wasted away. Eventually most of the imperial holdings were presented to their respective cities and opened to the public.

National interest in castles was renewed in 1928 when major castles and their remains were declared "important historical sites." The best of these were made "national treasures" under the patronage of the national government. In the 1930's some castles were rebuilt or renovated and restored. Some, such as Osaka Castle, were rebuilt with reinforced concrete, but they retained much of their original appearance. Others were restored using original materials wherever possible.

During the Pacific War eight castles were demolished by allied bombing, and the remains of many others were either destroyed or damaged. But as Japan's postwar economy began to recover, a virtual boom in castle rebuilding took place. The castle donjons that had been levelled were rebuilt of concrete in nearly exact replicas of the originals in outward appearance. Unfortunately some former castle towns have restored castle donjons that are of doubtful authenticity, and some cities have joined the boom by building castles where none existed before. Generally speaking, what remains of castle grounds are now public parks, and the rebuilt donjons are museums for the relics of the town's feudal past. Original castle donjons are not often used for this purpose, but they are generally open to the public and are of interest to students of construction and architecture.

III

Anatomy of the Japanese Castle

In feudal times, as we have seen, the daimyo's castle dominated the castle town, and its donjon was clearly visible at a great distance. Typically the castle was surrounded by an outer moat and earthworks. Its inner defenses consisted of moats, grass-covered and stone-faced ramparts, and stone walls topped with tile-roofed parapets; vulnerable areas were guarded by turrets. One passed through the walls by gates that led to inner courts separated from one another by stone-faced walls. The innermost court contained the main keep, the daimyo's palace, and the mansions of his chief retainers.

When choosing a site for castle construction several factors were considered. Foremost of these, of course, was that it be in a strategic location for control of the lines of communication in the area. Therefore most castles are found near the sea, navigable rivers, or on an important highway. Equally important were military considerations. The site selected included ideally a hill on which was built the main tower, affording a view of the surrounding plain for miles around in all directions. A nearby river or lake enhanced a potential site because the water could be diverted to fill moats and at the same time could be used as a natural obstacle in defense of the castle. Swamps and mud flats could also be used in much the same way.

Other considerations in site selection were convenience in governing the fief and location in respect to commercial activities. A site that was near the center of the fief made it possible to carry out administration of the domain more efficiently and effectively. A central location was also convenient for gathering products of the land for shipment to centers of consumption.

Because ideal castle sites are not found just anywhere, it is not surprising that a number of extant castles were built on or near locations that had been used as defensive positions for several centuries. For example, Gifu Castle is on a site that had been a defensive position as early as the 13th century; Edo Castle, built in the mid-15th century, was expanded into the largest castle in Japan during the early part of the 17th century; and Nagoya was built near the site of old Kiyosu Castle.

From a topographical standpoint there are three basic types of Japanese castles. The mountain castle or *san-jo*, which was noted in Chapter 1, typically stood on the summit of a mountain and originally was used as a subsidiary, rather than the primary, stronghold. It was important that the site be isolated from surrounding mountains to prevent the enemy from observing activities within the castle walls. If such a location were not available, castle builders selected a site that overlooked the surrounding territory on three sides and connected with a hill on the other. Natural obstacles such as cliffs, rocky terrain, and woods played a role in defending the stronghold. Besides advantages in defense, this type of castle was less vulnerable to earthquakes which are generally more destructive in plain areas. There were some disadvantages however: susceptibility to damage from high winds; relative inaccessibility to citizens of the fief; difficulties in building and in well digging for water supply.

Another type of castle is the *hira-jo* or castle on plain. This class of fortification was usually the home of the baron early in the feudal age. It was the seat of government, had a population center connected with it, and enjoyed the advantage of easy accessibility for the baron's subjects. However, it was more difficult to defend than the mountain type because it offered less natural protection, although rivers and swamps were often used to advantage and moats and earthworks were employed. Because there was little or no natural elevation on the site, only limited observation of the surrounding territory was possible. Often these castles were built in low areas to take advantage of a swamp for defense, but this sometimes boded well for the enemy who could divert a nearby river and flood out the castle. Also, because of the level site, the enemy was able to harass and observe the activities of the castle inmates by building siege towers. From these, the besiegers could see every move made within the castle and fire their weapons down on the defenders.

The third castle type is a combination of the other two. It is called the *hira-sanjo* or castle on plain and mountain, and had most of the advantages and few of the disadvantages of the others. The kind most often built after Hideyoshi ordered subsidiary castles torn down, this type typically was built on a small hill in the middle of a plain or on a low mountain overlooking a plain. The main tower was placed on the highest elevation surrounded by the inner portions of the castle. On the plain and lower hill stood the outer defenses.

The towns lay on the outskirts of the castles' fortifications. These, for the most part, were brand new cities, although many had grown up on the sites of small fishing or agricultural villages. The edicts commanding the warrior class to leave rural areas and move to castle towns stimulated their growth, with 50 to 80 percent of the population in these urban areas belonging to the samurai class. As the tide continued, merchants and artisans flocked to the towns to cater to the needs of the samurai. Welcomed because they contributed to the wealth of the domain, the merchants performed services to the daimyo during the civil wars. The artisans were valued because they produced the arms of war and the necessities of life. In spite of the initial rapid growth of these towns, however, long-term expansion was limited by their inability to produce economic goods or perform other economic functions. As shown in the previous chapter, the smaller fiefs that relied on agriculture for their economic base failed to grow beyond their ability to increase farm production.

The headquarters of Shinto shrines and Buddhist temples in the fiefs were also ordered moved to the castle towns, an order based on the former inclination of some priests and their followers to become revolutionary and resort to arms. By relocating them in the castle towns, the daimyo and their magistrates could keep priestly factions under surveillance.

The typical castle town was laid out so the streets were curved or so arranged as to prevent one from seeing down them for more than a few blocks. Such an arrangement was designed to confuse an invading enemy and to allow the defenders to carry out defensive operations unobserved. Tokyo was laid out in this manner until the great earthquake and fire of 1923 which virtually destroyed the city and permitted post-earthquake planners to design a grid system. Typical of the pattern are the castle towns of Hikone and Kanazawa, which have narrow, short streets.

Generally the quarters of the lesser samurai were on the outer edges of town. Next came the temples and shrines, the placement of which was not without military considerations. The large buildings of these establishments provided defensive positions for controlling major approaches to the town. They were therefore placed on the most vulnerable side of town and acted as a sort of barricade. The homes of the townspeople and merchants lay inside the temple-shrine cordon. Closer to the castle lived the middle-class samurai. The homes and shops of merchants under the daimyo's patronage were in the inner defense zone of the town, while surrounding the outer defenses of the castle proper were the homes of the greater samurai. This description of the composition and layout of the castle town is rather general. Each town differed somewhat from its counterparts because of variations in topographical situation, the individual defensive strategy of the daimyo, and the relative importance placed on the several classes of the town's inhabitants (Fig. 2).

Castle defenses consisted of moats, walls, fortified gates, corner turrets, strategically positioned courts, and towers. Occasionally, but not always, there was an outer moat that surrounded the town and an outer set of earthworks in a first line defense arrangement; frequently, however, the town itself was the outer line of defense. The defense of the castle proper began with a moat that was usually dug on the plain portion, but in some cases inner moats were constructed on the hill section as well. They were placed in areas not otherwise protected by such natural defenses as rivers or swamps.

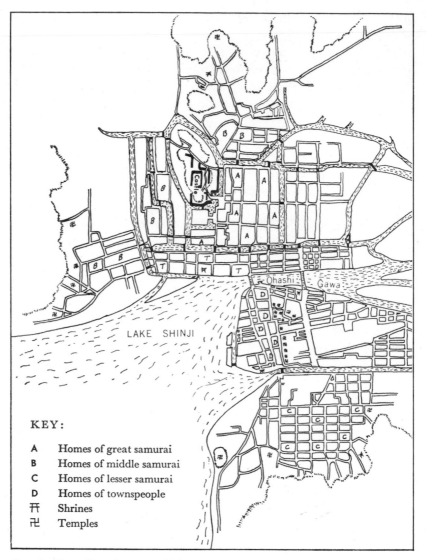

KEY:

A	Homes of great samurai
B	Homes of middle samurai
C	Homes of lesser samurai
D	Homes of townspeople
卉	Shrines
卍	Temples

FIG. 2. Plan of castle town of Matsue.

Moats varied in size, but the "standard" measurements were 65 feet wide and 20 feet deep. It was not uncommon, however, for some of them to exceed 330 feet in width, and it is said that at one time the moats at Osaka Castle were as wide as 360 feet and as deep as 24 feet. The moats were shaped in two basic pro-

38　CASTLES IN JAPAN

files—U and box. The former were constructed so that the walls met and supported each other like an inverted arch. The latter had a flat bottom and straight sides that were independent of each other. Often the sides were faced with stone to prevent erosive action of the water. Generally they were filled with water, thus creating a greater obstacle than if they had been dry. The water source varied, but most frequently it came from a nearby river that was diverted for the purpose. In other cases, however, as at Hikone and Matsue, water from a lake was used. Coastal castles, such as Takamatsu and Hagi, used sea water. Some moats were left dry and served as just another obstacle; this was especially true of castles located on rather high hills where it would have been extremely difficult to fill the moats and maintain the water level.

Immediately inside the moat stood the outer wall. Sometimes the wall was merely grass-covered earthern ramparts with a stone parapet as, for example, in parts of Edo Castle's defenses. More often, however, the outer wall was high and stone-faced. The wall surrounded the castle proper and was not used for protection of the town as was the case in European castles. The interior walls were also stone-faced and served to separate the several compounds from each other. Often in a mazelike arrangement with curves and turns, the walls could confuse the enemy who had penetrated the grounds and contain him in a small area where he would find it difficult to make a flank attack.

The wall had a core of earth that was usually obtained from excavation of the moats and leveling of the hill top. This core was faced with a layer of small pebbles or stones, topped by an outer surface made up of wedge-shaped stones of uncut or rough-hewed granite. Some of these stones are huge, and several used at Osaka are almost unbelievable. The small ends of the stones were placed on the outside of the wall, while the large ends faced inward; by arranging the stones in this manner, their weight tended to lock them together. Smaller stones were often forced between the larger ones to level and hold them in place. No mortar was used in the wall construction, with the result that adequate drainage was an inherent feature. The stones used on the corners were larger than those generally found in the wall proper and were usually well cut. They were fitted into place in much the same manner as bricks are laid (Figs. 3–6).

Concave in shape, the walls sloped at a 45-degree angle or more, some standing almost perpendicular. The shape was no doubt designed to withstand the water action in the moat, and is thought by some to derive from the grass-faced fortifications of ancient times. Both the shape and construction methods used in the walls were conceived to resist the destructive action of earthquakes. They usually measured 20 feet high (though many were much higher) and 50 feet thick at the base.

Many castle walls were equipped with a parapet from which the wall was defended (Fig. 7). It was constructed with a timber framework and was sometimes supported with timber buttresses. The sections between the framework were filled with clay mixed with salt, a combination that is very hard and durable if kept dry. The clay mixture was reinforced either with bamboo tied in place with twine or with wattled bamboo and straw. The surfaces were covered with white plaster, and a tile roof was provided to protect the top from becoming wet. Sometimes there were platforms at various places along the parapet so the defenders could throw stones and discharge arrows over the top of the wall. Another defensive device was stone-dropping chutes called *ishiotoshi,* a sort of window cut in the parapet from which stones, boiling water, and so forth could be dropped on the invader (Fig. 8). These openings had a cover on the outside of the parapet to protect the defenders from enemy fire. As we shall see later, this type of fixture was employed in some castle buildings as well. Round, rectangular, square, and triangular loopholes were usually built into the parapet (Fig. 9). The rectangular openings were used by archers, while defenders with firearms manned the others. Some parapets were on ground level, but others could be reached only by ramps or steps, some of which ran the full length of the wall so it could be defended quickly. Sometimes there were wide stairways at frequent intervals. These steps almost always ran parallel to the wall, but at Aizu-Wakamatsu there is a perpendicular pair of narrow steps (Figs. 10–12).

Frequently a one-story building along the top of the wall is integrated with, and serves the same purpose as, the parapet.

FIG. 3. Castle wall with corner tower and plastered parapet (Himeji Castle).

FIG. 4. Rough stone work on an outer wall (Himeji Castle).

FIG. 5. Detail of stone-faced walls. Well-cut stones of the inner court wall (Matsuyama Castle).

Fig. 6. The Octopus Stone, second largest at Osaka Castle. (The woman in the photo is five feet three inches tall.)

FIG. 7. Detail of parapet construction showing bamboo reinforcement, mud and straw fill, and exterior plaster covering, as well as a loophole (Matsuyama Castle).

FIG. 8. Well-cut wall corner stones. Note the ishiotoshi or stone-dropping chutes on the building above the wall (Himeji Castle).

FIG. 9. Variously shaped loopholes (Himeji Castle).

FIG. 10. Steps leading to parapets running the full length of the wall (Hagi Castle).

Fig. 11. Steps leading to parapets running along part of the wall (Himeji Castle).

FIG. 12. Perpendicular steps leading to the parapet (Wakamatsu Castle).

FIG. 13. Tamon or wall building (Himeji Castle).

FIG. 14. View of a masugata stripped of its parapets. The gap between the two walls once had a watariyagura (Wakamatsu Castle).

Fig. 15. Exterior view of a low, narrow interior gate designed to prevent observation from the outside (Himeji Castle).

Fig. 16. Interior view of a low, narrow gate designed to prevent observation from the outside (Himeji Castle).

FIG. 17. Hon-maru or inner court as viewed from the tenshu-kaku or main keep (Kochi Castle).

FIG. 18. Donjon foundation stones embedded in the earth-filled, stone-faced base (Hagi Castle).

Fig. 19. Roof tiles (Himeji Castle).

Fig. 20. Shachi, the mythical dolphin used to ward off fire and evil (Himeji Castle).

This is called a *tamon,* and it was used in several ways. The most frequent was the storage of arms and supplies, but sometimes it functioned as barracks, too. The tamon was provided with openings on the outer side for discharging weapons, and it sometimes had ishiotoshi as well. Entrance was through doors from the court. This type of structure could also provide a protected connection between various sections of the castle (Fig. 13).

Towers or turrets, usually one to three stories (some were higher), were built on the corner of walls. Their primary purpose was for observation and to protect vulnerable portions of the wall as well as to provide a secure place for directing fire upon the enemy. They also had ishiotoshi overhanging the wall. Some castles had "moon-viewing" turrets, a terminology indicating that these towers were used for pleasure as well as for war.

To enter the castle and its various courts one crossed the moats via a causeway or bridge and, as mentioned earlier in this chapter, passed through numerous gates. The causeways, called *dobashi,* were made of earth and placed across the moat at points where the enemy would be in a vulnerable position. Wooden bridges were also employed in moat crossings. In some cases they were drawbridges of both the hung and the withdrawable types, while others were the regular wooden variety but were walled and roofed. Occasionally there was a combination of causeway and bridge crossing.

Japanese castles had at least two gates—front and rear—and usually many more. The main gate was called *ote-mon, ote* meaning "big hand" and *mon* meaning "gate." It was here that opposing forces usually met in a frontal clash. *Sakura-mon* or cherry-blossom gate was a name commonly given to a secondary gate at many castles, and other gates were named after the district of the castle town in their vicinity or for individuals, animals, or the enclosures they guarded. The rear gate was called *karamete* (binding gate), and it was here that prisoners were taken and the defenders sallied out to attack the enemy. The most common type of gate was the *masugata* or measuring gate which derives its name from a measuring vessel called *masu.* This kind of gate was actually two gates in one, with one facing the outside of the castle and the other opening to the inside. Entering the masugata, the visitor

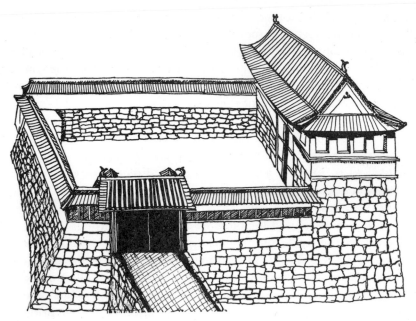

F<small>IG</small>. 21. Sketch of a masugata or "measuring gate" with the watariyagura shown on the right.

passed through the rather narrow outer gate that usually had a tiled roof. Once inside, he found himself in a court surrounded by a wall on three sides and a much larger gate placed at right-angles to the first on the fourth side. The inner gate was a two-story affair with a form of tamon comprising the second floor. This combination is called a *watariyagura,* meaning a tower that bridges both sides, because it was located between two walls. It was this structure that formed the main defense of the gate; from the tower, the defenders could fire down on the attackers, and the floor boards could be removed and objects dropped on the would-be-invaders attempting to batter down the gate (Figs. 14, 21).

Among the many advantages of this kind of defense was the impossibility for outsiders to observe activities within the castle walls because there was no straight line of sight through the gate.

At the same time troops could go in or out of the castle without the risk of opening both gates at once. They could assemble in the court between the gates while one gate was closed and the other opened. (The standard masugata was designed to hold 240 foot soldiers or 40 mounted men.) Another factor was the difficulty any invader would encounter in storming the gate and finding a 90-degree turn between the two entrances and a limited space in the court area.

Gates between the various courts were usually of the masugata type, but frequently there were low, narrow gates that were designed to prevent the enemy from observing movements through them from a vantage point such as a siege tower (Figs. 15, 16). The ground level just inside the gate usually sloped upwards, and almost immediately inside there was a right-angle turn similar to the masugata. After the turn, there was a steeply sloped narrow passage into the next court. Should this type of gate be stormed, defense of the position would have been aided by the intruder's difficulty in negotiating the turn and slopes while fending off the attack by the defenders.

The masugata gateway itself was closed by massive folding doors made of heavy timbers. They were often bound with iron straps and were sometimes plated with copper or iron. The doors were held shut with a wooden beam placed in iron brackets, and the hinges were made to take the blows of battering rams. Usually on one side of the gateway there was a smaller opening for individuals or small groups when the main gate was closed.

The courts or baileys, called *kuruwa*, were concentric in arrangement with the center on the highest ground. The layout, however, was somewhat different in each castle due to differences in site location and the defensive strategy of the builder. They were placed in such a way that if one compound were captured it could be retaken from another line of defense. A mazelike arrangement made it difficult for the whole castle to be overpowered at one time, for the enemy found himself surrounded by walls when he entered a court where he could be fired upon from all sides. This kind of defense is sometimes called a "watertight compartment" because, for all practical purposes, it was sealed (Fig. 22).

The main court, where the donjon or keep was situated, was called the *hon-maru*, the word *maru* referring to something that is round. The second and third compounds were called *ni-no-maru* and *san-no-maru* respectively, while other courts were given various names but were usually known by the points of the compass where they were located. Thus there was sometimes a *nishi* (west) or *kita* (north) maru. It was not unusual to find a court set aside for committing suicide, used for that purpose when all was lost in battle or by disgraced samurai in peace time.

The courts were endowed with scenic landscaping. The gardens of the hon-maru were laid out for the pleasure of the daimyo, but the landscaping in general served purposes other than aesthetic. Rows of trees, usually evergreens, were planted directly behind many of the walls in order to screen activities within the castle. At the same time, these trees served as a shield from incoming missiles fired by the enemy. On the slopes of the castle hill near the outer defenses it was not unusual to find a virtual forest designed to veil activities of the defenders. Other plants and trees also provided war materials in the event of a prolonged siege. Bamboo could be cut and used for arrow shafts, and oaks were available for spear shafts. In addition to wells, garden ponds could supply emergency water reserves.

The palace of the daimyo was usually located in the hon-maru, although in some instances his home was outside, but near, the castle grounds. The palace was often elaborately decorated with fine carvings, rich woods, and the works of famous artists. Frequently the floorboards of the palace were laid so they would make considerable noise when walked upon, thus discouraging intruders from sneaking through private areas of the palace without making their presence known. Flooring of this type is known as *uguisu-bari* or nightingale boarding. Within the hon-maru or other inner courts of the castle stood the mansions of the chief retainers, while the outer courts generally were reserved for defensive purposes.

Inside the hon-maru was the *tenshu-kaku* or main tower keep (Figs. 17, 24), a massive structure some three to seven stories high usually located on the highest ground available. Often it served as one of the corner towers of the inner court. Depending upon

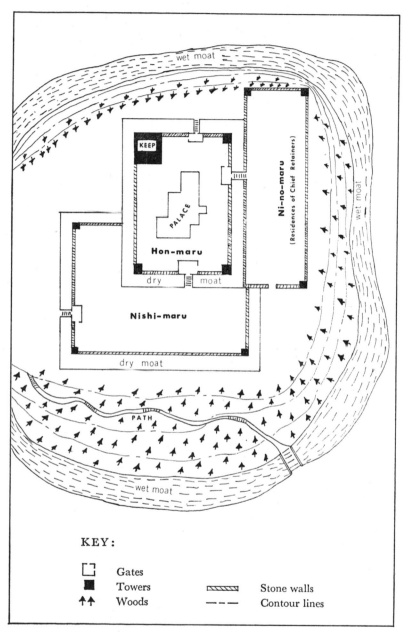

Labels within the figure:

wet moat

KEEP

PALACE

Hon-maru

Ni-no-maru
(Residences of Chief Retainers)

dry   moat

Nishi-maru

dry moat

PATH

wet moat

KEY:

Gates

Towers

Woods

Stone walls

Contour lines

FIG. 22. Typical castle plan.

the castle's design, the donjon was either an independent structure or was connected to lesser towers by a type of tamon or by underground passages. The main keep served several purposes. A reminder to the fief population of the daimyo's power, it was at the same time the principal arsenal. In time of war it functioned as the main observation and command post, affording an excellent view of the surrounding area. It was the living quarters of the daimyo and his chief retainers during periods of siege, and if the rest of the castle fell, the donjon was the final line of defense.

The base of the donjon was of well-hewn, closely fitted stone (as compared to the rather rough stonework of the walls), and had about the same contour as the wall. Often the base was a fairly high structure because the remainder of the tower was primarily of wood construction and could be set afire by an enemy if it were within easy reach. This stone structure frequently was used as a basement for the donjon, but in some cases it was filled with earth (Fig. 18).

The main tower supports rested upon large foundation stones in the base and extended upward for several floors, occasionally continuing all the way to the top floor to give the structure stability. From these supports, platforms were built to form the various floors of the tower, and supports for other floors were added as needed. These supports were not necessarily of a single board. Instead, several planks were sometimes laminated together with large iron staples and fairly light-weight iron straps. Pillars and cross beams were joined by a mortise and tenon technique where the tenon of the beam passed through the pillar and was held in place with a wedge key. This made the framework sturdy, yet allowed it to be flexible enough to withstand the frequent earthquakes that shake the country.

The exterior of the donjon was usually treated in the same manner as the parapet—that is, made of timbers, a clay-salt mixture, and finished with a coating of plaster. Some donjons, however, were finished in wood and frequently were painted black, as at Kumamoto, Hiroshima, and Okayama. A well to provide water in time of siege was generally dug in the basement. In some of the earlier modern-day castles the upper floors of the donjon were elaborately decorated because the tower was used as the living quarters of the war lord, but as the daimyo began to live in palaces, the interior of the keep was left unfinished with the beams and supports exposed. Very steep stairways were placed between floors, and often there were low clearances between the cross beams (occasionally the modern-day visitor will see the warning, "mind your head," when making his way on these stairs). On various floors in some castles there were elevated platforms around the walls, used by soldiers as positions from which to fire upon the enemy through the windows.

The top floor of the main tower keep was for observation, and in time of war it was the command post for the daimyo. Because of this function, it had openings on all four sides with the fortuitous side effect of good lighting and ventilation. To aid observation there was frequently a balcony all the way around. Since the daimyo used this floor, it was made relatively comfortable with *tatami* mats on the floor (these are grass mats, three feet by six in size; the area of a room is stated in terms of the number of mats).

The external appearance of the donjon is usually characteristic of the Azuchi-Momoyama period of architectural design, the roof lines being the most distinguishable feature. The triangular *chidori-hafu* gable with a slight curve combined with the *kara-hafu*, a curved gable of Chinese style, give the donjon a majestic and aesthetic profile. The number of eaves does not necessarily indicate the number of stories within the structure because there are often two floors between them. The donjon profile tapers from bottom to top, with each succeeding floor-eave set being smaller than the one below it. Windows are of two basic designs: the *katomado*, a bell-shaped opening, and the *renji*. The latter is rectangular in shape with vertical slats that were designed to give protection from enemy fire and provide the defenders with openings for discharging their weapons.

Roofs of most castle buildings and parapets were covered with semicircular tiles (pantiles) that were alternately inverted and overlapped and were sealed at the seams with lime mortar. The last tile on each row, the end tile, had a round face that usually bore the crest of the castle owner. On the ends of the ridge line there was a pair of mythical dolphins (called *shachi*), charms against fire and evil. They were made either of tile or metal and were sometimes gilded with gold (Figs. 19, 20).

Besides the main tower, some castles had one or more secondary towers. Useful for observation, they also could protect wells, confine prisoners, or provide another sanctuary for committing suicide if the need arose. Other castle buildings included godowns, stables, and powder magazines.

IV

Four Major Castles

◈ **Azuchi Castle**

Prior to the introduction of firearms most castles were built with 10 foot-high earthen walls that had loopholes for bows and arrows. The castles were generally located in places that were difficult to approach because of their natural surroundings. As we have seen, many feudal barons had two strongholds—one that was used as a combination residence, government house, and fortress, and another in the mountains for use in crisis situations.

The introduction of firearms into Japan by the Portuguese in 1542, and their rapid adoption by the various barons, made the old-style fortification somewhat obsolete.[1] Azuchi Castle, as mentioned earlier, was the prototype of the kind of castle that was to be built in the future as a defense against these new arms. It was started in 1576 by Nobunaga and was completed in 1579 after $3\frac{1}{2}$ years of work.[2] Built on a point of land jutting into Lake Biwa about 30 miles from Kyoto, it stood on a hill overlooking a plain and controlled vital lines of communications to the capital.[3] Constructed primarily as a stronghold, the castle was used by Nobunaga as a residence while he consolidated his control over the country. It was erected on a high road (Nakasendo) and provided him with much-needed protection from his enemies.

65

The castle, which was built to plans reportedly supplied by the Portuguese, was a massive structure compared to other strongholds of the day. A small army of men worked around the clock inching huge stones up the hill called Azuchiyama to the construction site.[4] On the lakeside, protection was afforded by cliffs rising as high as 660 feet above the water. On the unprotected sides deep moats and a stone wall 70 feet high and "several" thousand feet long, were built.[5] Within the outer defenses stood four citadels, each within the other, each irregular in shape so as to confuse an attacker should he break through the outer walls. The tower was some seven stories or 170 feet high. The massive stone foundation alone was 70 feet high and formed the first floor. The first floor reportedly measured 120 by 102 feet, had a total of 60 iron-covered openings to provide light, and contained some 45 rooms.

Although nothing remains of the original keep (except the stone foundation), Nobunaga's secretary left a very detailed description. The second floor contained several ornate rooms with painted decorations of various human and wild life. One room was 12 mats in size with gold-covered walls and decorated with plum blossoms. This floor was also used as a storage area for such essentials as ammunition, food, and clothing. The third floor was about 100 mats large and consisted of many chambers. The fourth had a landscaped garden, complete with rocks and trees, a hand-ball court, and more detailed paintings. The fifth floor had no paintings, but the sixth included four octagonal rooms with the exterior pillars lacquered red and interior pillars lacquered gold. The top floor, which served as an observation platform, featured an 18-mat room, decorated with gold leaf and paintings of dragons. The Jesuit priest, Luis Foris, also gives us a description of the castle in general.* He says the houses of Nobunaga's vassals were decorated with gold and roofed with bluish tile. Lookout towers, manned day and night, were situated

---

* The remarks of Foris and three other early visitors to Japan, Caron, Saris, and de Vivero y Velasco, who appear later in the book, come from Michael Cooper's *They Came to Japan: An Anthology of European Reports on Japan, 1543–1640.*

on the walls. The main walls were covered with skillfully wrought iron, and the stables were kept so clean that they would have been fit habitation for nobles of high rank. Within the castle's outer wards stood the mansions of Nobunaga's chief vassals, along with various storehouses and even a temple to cater to the religious needs of his men.

Azuchi Castle had several distinct features that differentiated it from its predecessors. Its massive proportions and the use of stone as a major building material, as noted in an earlier chapter, were to provide protection from the most destructive firearms available at that time. Other innovations such as the use of high towers and the location of the castle on a hill rather than in mountains with dense vegetation, were also related to a change in the tactics of warfare. These changes made guns an extremely effective defense because the enemy could be seen a long way off and met by gunfire precisely directed from the height of the donjon.

Just as Azuchi Castle was the prototype of the present-day relics of feudal times, the castle town created by Nobunaga outside the castle walls was the prototype of a new kind of castle town in general. He had built quarters for his various soldiers and retainers but they were slow to occupy them, and it was two or three years before the town became fairly well settled.[6] At the same time, he made conditions attractive for tradesmen and artisans so that the town would be supplied with the necessary commodities to make it prosper. In 1577 Nobunaga issued a town charter stating that Azuchi was to be a free-market town with no taxes levied on sales or purchases. All merchants traveling along the Nakasendo had to seek lodging in the town when passing through, there were to be no taxes on building or transportation (except in time of war), and in the event of cancellation of debts in the province, debts owed to the town's residents would not be included. These concessions to tradesmen were made to attract money to the town, but the motive was more political than economic. With free trade, goods flowed from all parts of the country to the population and market centers, thus increasing the wealth of the cities and in turn the lord of the area. At the same time, the roads were improved to facilitate the movement of goods, and in time of war the same roads could be used to move troops. Free-trade practices also attracted skilled artisans whose talents could be used to make the tools of war.[7]

It was during this period that Jesuit missionaries arrived in Japan and received encouragement from Nobunaga, who regarded them as a rival to Buddhism for which he had little use. When Father Gnecchi Organtino and some other priests visited Nobunaga at Azuchi, Nobunaga was so flattered that he offered the Jesuits a building site for both a church and a house; the missionaries were only too happy to accept.

After Akechi Mitsuhide killed Nobunaga at Kyoto on June 21, 1582 he marched to Azuchi, took over the castle, and distributed gifts from Nobunaga's treasury to likely supporters.[8] He did no harm to the castle, but Azuchi nevertheless met its downfall shortly thereafter. It is known for certain that the fortress burned to the ground, but by whom is open to controversy. One popular and often repeated story is that Nobunaga's son, in a fit of rage, grief, or perhaps both, put the castle to the torch. Sansom acknowledges the story, but indicates that looting townspeople probably were responsible for the fire.[9] Still another version says that the tower was destroyed by Nobunaga's adversaries. In any case, the castle burned, leaving only the stone walls, moats, earthworks, and tower foundation (Fig. 23).

The town of Azuchi is now a country village populated by people (some of whom are direct descendants of Nobunaga) who till the land, fish in Lake Biwa, and are proud of their history. At one time they wanted to rebuild the castle donjon but the idea was abandoned for several reasons including lack of funds. Also, the remains of the castle have been declared a special historical relic, and the Committee for the Preservation of Cultural Assets is reluctant to allow construction of a new donjon because of possible damage to the ruins. In addition there is some question whether reliable plans and drawings exist from which a reasonable facsimile could be built. Proponents of the project claim that drawings of the original castle exist and are the property of a temple at the foot of Azuchiyama, but the only known evidence of drawings is a sketch of the exterior on a scroll hanging in the temple.

◆ Osaka Castle

The Castle of Osaka was at one time the mightiest in all Japan, second only to the fortress at Edo in size and magnificence. Although it was by no means an architectural monument, as were the cathedrals of Europe, it rivaled any Western structure in size and materials used (Fig. 24). The ideal site on which the castle stood in the delta of the Yodo River was surrounded on three sides by rivers and overlooked a flat area on the west that stretched to the sea. Recognizing the site's security, the early Japanese emperors Ojin (d. 310 A.D.) and Nintoku (d. 399 A.D.) are said to have built palaces on the hill that is now the castle site.

In 1496 the Ikko Buddhists constructed a temple called Ishi-yama Honganji on the castle site. Members of this sect were fanatics who, through contributions from the faithful, became wealthy and, as mentioned before, built strong military forces. By Nobunaga's time this formidable group was his single strongest rival for absolute power. Because of the temple's location, it became a virtual fortress which Nobunaga found to be practically impregnable. And, since it was easy to supply from the sea and rivers, it was almost impossible to starve out unless there was no external support. Nobunaga tried several times to lay siege to the fortress, but each time was forced to withdraw because of more urgent demands on his resources. These demands, however, finally helped him to take the fortress because he had defeated many of the sect's outside supporters. At the same time he changed his tactics against the bastion, first overrunning its various inland strongholds, then attacking the main fort. In following this plan, he gathered his forces in Kyoto in 1577 and began to sweep through neighboring provinces, thus isolating the Ikko sect from any remaining support it may have had. As the siege went on, the crowded fortress inmates began to run short of supplies, and the elderly, women, and children attempted to escape on a stormy night. The next morning a junk full of human noses and ears floated past the fortress, affording the besieged a morbid report on the success of the escape.

The Ikko fortresses consisted of five interconnected strongholds, three of which were captured by Nobunaga's forces in the course of the siege. During the battle for the remaining forts many defenders were killed, and it is said that the stench of burning bodies filled the air for miles around. At last, as noted before, the emperor interceded and effected the surrender of the fortress in May 1580.

In the autumn of 1583 Hideyoshi began building a castle where the old temple had stood. Some 30,000 men toiled on the construction day and night watched by supervisors, each of whom was responsible for the work in a certain area. According to contemporary accounts, anyone falling behind schedule was subject to exile and loss of his estates. A large number of stones was required to build this mighty fortress, and the lords for miles around were obliged to supply them. For instance, the city of Sakai (a fortified mercantile city) reportedly gave 200 vessels full of stone a day. In all a total of more than 1,000 ships, each ferrying large cargoes of stone, arrived each day.[10]

After three years of work the finished castle was designated the seat of government for the country. It was here that Ieyasu submitted to Hideyoshi, and it was from here that the Odawara and Korean Campaigns were directed. It was in this castle, also, that Hideyoshi received the Chinese delegation during the Korean conflict after an earthquake had destroyed Fushimi Castle and had greatly damaged all but a quakeproof corner tower at Osaka.

At the height of its glory, Osaka Castle boasted an eight-story, 102-foot-high tower that stood on a 75-foot stone base. In addition there were 48 large and 76 smaller corner towers. The defenses consisted of two courts, one surrounding the other, each protected by a moat. The inner court could not be entered without crossing over both of these barriers. In total size, the castle was almost eight miles in circumference and was more than 187 acres in area. It measured some 1.4 miles east to west and 1.2 miles north to south. The second moat varied in size from 80 to 120 yards wide and 12 to 23 feet deep, while the inner moat was 240 feet wide, 36 feet deep, and the water varied in depth from 12 to 24 feet.

Perhaps the most remarkable aspect of the castle was the size of some of the stones used in building its walls. The largest of these is called the Higo-*ishi* (furnished by the Lord of Higo) which measures 47.6 feet long and 19.2 feet high and is located inside the ote-mon or front gate of the castle. Another large stone is the *taiko-ishi* or Drum Rock (also known as the Octopus Stone, Fig. 6), just inside the Sakura Gate, measuring 18.9 feet high and 36.6 feet long. The stones bear the seal of the feudal lord who donated them.[11] These huge granite stones are said to have been quarried at Shodoshima and shipped through the Inland Sea.

In September 1593 Hideyoshi's mistress, Yodo, gave birth to a son and heir who was eventually named Hideyori. Since Hideyoshi intended that his heir should have Osaka Castle, he built Fushimi near Kyoto to use in his retirement and died there on September 18, 1598. After his death, the Osaka Castle remained the home of the child, Hideyori, but Ieyasu stayed there from time to time, thus contravening the rules Hideyoshi had issued before his death. Ieyasu spent the first few months of 1600 there, during which time the Englishman, Will Adams, was shipwrecked on the shores of Japan and saw Ieyasu at the castle. A month or two later, Ieyasu received word of an open revolt signaling the beginning of a chain of events that led to the battle at Sekigahara, described in Chapter 2.

Osaka remained the power center for the Toyotomi Clan, with Hideyori and his mother living there under the guardianship of one Katagiri. The latter had led Ieyasu to believe that Hideyori was rather slow-witted, but an interview with Hideyori at Kyoto's Nijo Castle in 1611 convinced Ieyasu that Hideyori was anything but stupid. That interview probably sealed the young man's fate. Ieyasu decided that the House of Toyotomi had to be destroyed to remove it as a threat to the Tokugawa dynasty.

Prior to this Ieyasu had encouraged Hideyori and his mother to build numerous shrines and temples to perpetuate the memory of Hideyoshi. Far from sentiment, Ieyasu's motive was to reduce the wealth of the family. One of these building projects included a bell with an inscription that offended Ieyasu because it seemed to imply that the House of Tokugawa was inferior to the Toyotomi. In September 1614 Katagiri visited Ieyasu at Shizuoka (Sumpu) to try to repair the differences between the two houses. Yodo also sent a delegation of her ladies-in-waiting to offer her apologies for any offense that had been taken. The ladies were graciously received by Ieyasu who did not mention the bell but merely asked that Hideyori refrain from making preparations for war (he had received reports that this was taking place). On the other hand Ieyasu did not receive Katagiri, informing him through a retainer that Hideyori must be brought into line and that an apology was expected for the bell inscription.

On the way back to Osaka, Katagiri and the ladies met and compared notes. He suggested that the best way to avoid trouble was for either Hideyori or Yodo to go to Edo as a hostage, at least until Ieyasu passed away (he was over 70 years of age), after which the Toyotomi forces might have a better chance to make a bid for power. The ladies suspected Katagiri of treason for this suggestion since their experience with Ieyasu had indicated no hostility. Reaching Osaka before Katagiri, they told of their suspicions, whereupon Katagiri, shortly after his arrival, was forced under threat to retire to his estates.

With Katagiri out of the way no insulation remained between the two houses, and a confrontation was inevitable. Records at the English factory at Hirado show that the Tokugawa probably decided as early as June 1614 to battle the Osaka forces. At that time gun powder was quickly bought up at Shizuoka, and on the same order the English sold Ieyasu four Culverine cannons capable of throwing a 13-pound shot and one Shaker that was a little lighter in weight but could fire a 23-pound shot. Not until October did the Osaka forces became concerned enough to prepare for their defenses, and by then gunpowder had become scarce, and the English had difficulty filling the orders from Osaka.

About this time an appeal went out to those who had suffered at Sekigahara to join in the support of the House of Toyotomi. The appeal drew many ronin (masterless samurai), and within a week 90,000 had entered the castle. Less successful was the campaign to recruit daimyo who had once been loyal supporters of the House, for only 14 (out of 197) now sympathized with the Osaka cause, and all of them had hostages at Edo. Some of Hideyori's commanders had proposed taking the offensive immediately by seizing the towns of Oji, Fushimi, and Kyoto, thus blocking the Tokugawa advance and taking physical possession of the emperor. With the emperor under their protection, they would have him proclaim the Tokugawa a rebel and induce sympathetic daimyo to join the Osaka camp. Hideyori counterproposed that his forces remain at the castle, take up defensive positions, and wait for the attack there; this plan was accepted.

In the meantime, Ieyasu had obtained written professions of loyalty from the daimyo of 50 western provinces and began to mobilize his forces. The various western daimyo were ordered to dispatch troops to the Osaka area and were assigned positions in an irregular curve some 15 to 30 miles from the city. By December 10 the Eastern forces had arrived at Fushimi and were ready to move on to Osaka. The Western troops had been advancing in the meantime, and had had several skirmishes with the Osaka supporters.

The Eastern forces moved from Fushimi and took up positions south of the castle. While these troops waited, the Western armies captured most of the remaining areas around the bastion after some severe fighting and considerable loss. By December 29 all of Hideyori's outposts had been subdued and all efforts were concentrated on the castle itself; the siege was on. Ieyasu ordered scaling ladders made for a possible assault, had siege towers built, and caused the castle to be bombarded for three consecutive days in the evening and at dawn. At the same time, miners attempted to undermine the castle towers, while archers practiced psychological warfare by sending messages to the defenders, urging them to take the wisest course of action and surrender. There were several earnest attempts to overrun various positions held by the defenders, but the battle soon ended in a stalemate.

Finding the castle nearly impregnable, Ieyasu next attempted to use bribery and diplomacy to accomplish his end. First he tried to bribe several of the defenders to allow him entry to the castle but all attempts failed. Next he sent for Ocha no Tsubone, who was a good friend of Yodo's sister, to act as a go-between in diplomatic negotiations. In order to "prepare" Yodo for peace talks, the castle was bombarded during the night of January 16 (1615) so that the defenders (especially the ladies) would get little sleep.[12] At the same time war cries were sounded at various times along with sudden volleys of shots to give the impression that an attack was imminent. The next morning, just as Yodo was about to take tea with her ladies, a 13-pound shot landed in her apartment within the main keep. The panic that followed caused Yodo to ask two of Hideyori's generals to urge him to sue for peace, but this idea was rejected by the other generals.

Ieyasu also sent a Kyoto merchant, Goto Shosaburo, to the castle with two alternative propositions for the defenders. One was that Yodo go to Edo as hostage to insure good behavior on the part of the defenders. The other alternative was that the castle be rendered useless by allowing the moats and walls to be destroyed so that it would no longer be a threat to the House of Tokugawa. Hideyori was also offered a new fief in the provinces of Kazusa and Awa (near Edo).[13] The latter was flatly refused, and Hideyori countered with a request for a fief of two provinces in Shikoku; this request was rejected by Ieyasu.

On January 18, the anniversary of Hideyoshi's death, one of Ieyasu's generals felt certain that Hideyori would pay a call at the shrine in the castle to pay respects to his father's memory. The general, Katagiri Katsumoto, stationed at the Kyobashi Gate, fired a shot aimed at the shrine when it was thought Hideyori would be there. The shot missed its mark and landed in the unfortunate Yodo's apartment, killing two of her ladies-in-waiting.

About this time representatives of both sides met to attempt to bring the opposing forces to terms. Ieyasu's spokesman promised that no harm was meant to Hideyori, that he would be free to stay at the castle with no reduction of revenue, and that his men were free to leave the bastion if they wished with no reprisals. Ieyasu only asked that the outermost defenses be destroyed as a token of goodwill. Yodo's sister, one of the negotiators, was also shown the progress of the miners who were digging under the moat toward the inner part of the castle, and was told to report what she saw to Yodo. The report on the miners, plus the wayward shot that landed in her apartment that morning, were all that Yodo needed to persuade Hideyori and his generals to conclude hostilities. On January 19 final agreement was reached.

Ieyasu departed for Kyoto on January 24, leaving his son Hidetada, the shogun, to see to filling in the outer moat and leveling the outer rampart. The work was completed in a very few days, and, much to the distress of Yodo, part of the inner defenses were also destroyed. Protests were directed to one of Ieyasu's representatives, but to little avail. Yodo then appealed to another Ieyasu aide, who said he was too ill to do anything at the time but would put a stop to the destruction as soon as he recovered. Strangely enough, it took an abnormally long time for him to get over his malady, and by then all that remained of the castle was the main citadel. When the aide finally was able to visit the castle, he appeared surprised at what had happened. It was a pity, he said, that such destruction had been permitted, but what was done, was done, and redigging the inner moat would be far too expensive. Besides, peace had been restored and there was no need for elaborate defenses. On February 16 the job of destroying the outer defenses was complete, just 26 days after it had begun. Thus ended the Winter Campaign, as this incident is known in Japanese history.

It was only about a month later that Hideyori began recruiting ronin again. Through various spies, Ieyasu learned that: (1) ronin were gathering from throughout the provinces; (2) the defenders were split into several factions, and Yodo often interfered; (3) councils of war occurred frequently but accomplished nothing; (4) Hideyori's men were redigging the moats and constructing stockades and other defensive works. Ieyasu then ordered Hideyori to vacate the castle and remove himself to another fief (where this domain was located has not been recorded). Apparently the Osaka forces rejected the order, for on May 3 Ieyasu left Shizuoka for Kyoto to deal with the problem, stopping long enough at Nagoya to attend the wedding of his ninth son, Yoshinao. He then proceeded to Kyoto, arriving there on May 17, and on the 20th or 21st, his son Hidetada arrived with the Eastern Army.

On May 24 the shogun's forces, about 220,000 strong, began to converge on the castle. The plan was for them to take up positions approximately the same as they had occupied during the Winter Campaign. The fortress they faced this time was not nearly so impregnable as it had been before. The men defending the weakened castle probably numbered 60,000 ronin and 120,000 household troops, many of whom suffered from considerable unrest due to internal strife.[14]

While the Tokugawa forces were moving from Kyoto to Osaka, Hideyori's generals began offensive action. On May 28, 2,000 troops advanced into Yamato, set fire to several towns, threatened Nara, and burned the mercantile city of Sakai. On June 1 the Osaka forces attempted to block the Eastern Army's advance but were overwhelmed by superior numbers. Although they were forced to withdraw, they did so after inflicting considerable casualties on some of the advancing forces. Thus began what is called the Summer Campaign.

By June 2 the Eastern forces had taken up positions around the castle with the Tokugawa forces facing it on the south. At the same time the Osaka forces held a council of war and decided to do battle the next day on the open ground south of the castle. One group of forces was to move through the city streets and attack the Tokugawa army from the rear. The besieging forces, thrown into confusion from this maneuver, would then be confronted with a frontal assult by contingents of ronin. At the height of the battle, Hideyori was to put in a dramatic appearance at the head of his household troops and sweep away the enemy before him.

The final battle for the castle began at noon on June 3. The rear-attack force was discovered and held in check, but the forces near the castle started their direct attack and were quite successful in putting to rout the front line of the enemy—had it not been for adequate reserves and superior numbers, the day might have been lost for the Tokugawa. During the heat of the battle, forces led by Asano of Wakayama on the Tokugawa left flank made an unexpected advance that appeared to be an act of desertion to the Echizen forces on their right. This movement threw the Echizen forces into panic, who broke ranks and ran into the center of the line. Order was soon restored, and by two o'clock the main body of the Osaka force had retreated to the castle.

There was treachery within the castle walls during and after the battle. Hideyori failed to leave the castle with his troops at the critical time because of his fear that traitors would set it afire in his absence.[15] Also, one of his generals, Hayami, urged him not to expose himself to open battle, but rather to save himself for the defense of the castle. The final blow came when a cook set fire to his kitchen and the flames, fanned by a brisk wind, spread throughout the enclosure. While the situation was one of confusion within, the besieging forces increased their efforts and finally gained entrance to the second enclosure; by five o'clock this area was controlled by the invaders.

In the meantime, Hayami moved Hideyori, his mother, and his wife to a fireproof building for their protection. While the final battle was waged, Hideyori's wife, who was Ieyasu's granddaughter, was sent to beg that the lives of her husband and mother-in-law be spared. The request was rejected and she returned to the castle.[16] Hideyori's eight-year-old son, Kunimatsu, was sought out and beheaded so that no Toyotomi would remain to challenge the authority of the House of Tokugawa in the future. On June 4 the House of Toyotomi was finally destroyed when Hideyori committed suicide and Yodo was beheaded by one of their retainers at Yamazato Kuruwa (Hill Close) behind the main tower.

The defenders met their fate in various ways. Of course many were killed in the battle, but others, most notably the leaders, committed suicide. For the many ronin captured alive, Ieyasu devised a grisly fate. It was felt necessary to annihilate these men to help insure future peace in the country. They were beheaded, and their heads were paraded all the way between Fushimi and Kyoto. Missionaries who witnessed the scene reported that the heads were stuck on planks and there were 18 rows, some of which had over a thousand heads.

After 1615, Osaka was no longer an important military center, but became one of the three chief cities under direct control of the shogunate.[17] A 10-year restoration of the castle was begun in 1620, but the donjon was struck by lightning and destroyed in 1665. During the remainder of the feudal period the castle grounds served as the seat of local government and for the garrisoning of troops.

As time went on, Osaka became the most important commercial center in the country. Hideyoshi had encouraged merchants from the fortified city of Sakai to move to Osaka and supply the castle and the town, which was rapidly growing. After Ieyasu took over, more merchants came in from Fushimi. Although the daimyo of the Ou and Kanto districts built warehouses in Edo to store and distribute their revenues of rice, most of the feudal lords converted rice into cash at Osaka. Soon there were some 500 to 600 warehouses in the city which not only processed food, but many other forms of merchandise as well.

During most of the Tokugawa period the city remained a peaceful but busy commercial center. In 1837, however, the peace was broken by a riot led by one Oshio Heihachiro. Many fires were started, and homes and buildings (especially of the rich) were destroyed before troops garrisoned at the castle could bring the situation under control. This riot was an overt expression of national dissatisfaction with the government, a malcontent feeling that eventually led to the downfall of the Tokugawa regime. During the 1850's and '60's the castle was used to receive foreign diplomats when the shogun was in residence there.

In September 1868 part of the castle was burned by Tokugawa troops as they retreated before troops loyal to the emperor during the civil war that brought about the Restoration. In 1931 a donjon of ferro-concrete material was constructed atop the 45-foot foundation of the former keep, and the castle grounds were opened as a public park. During the Pacific War troops were again garrisoned on the castle grounds. Although the new donjon was not touched by the war, four turrets were destroyed. Today the castle grounds are again used as a public park, and the donjon contains exhibits relating to the history of old Osaka including a display of archeological interest and a model of the castle showing what it was like at its prime.

◈ Fushimi Castle

Fushimi Castle, briefly mentioned in Chapter 2, was built by Hideyoshi between 1594 and 1596 (there are some indications that it may have been started in 1592), and was a plain-and-mountain type of fortification. The hill on which it stood is now called Momoyama or Peach Hill because about 100 years after the castle was destroyed a peach orchard was planted on the site.

Several reasons have been given as to why Hideyoshi built Fushimi, and at least four of them seem to be valid. First there was the need to defend Kyoto in the south. The city is protected to some extent by mountains on all sides except in the direction of Fushimi. Besides this, the site was near enough to Osaka (25 miles) for signal fires to be visible between the two cities. Another reason for building the castle, as mentioned earlier, was to provide a residence for Hideyoshi upon his retirement. He had given his mansion, Jurakudai, to his adopted son, and Osaka Castle was to be turned over to Hideyori. Also, Hideyoshi wanted to use the castle to impress the representatives from China, a country he was planning to subjugate upon the anticipated success of the Korean Campaign.[18] Finally, he planned to reduce the wealth of the northeastern daimyo by making them contribute heavily to the castle's construction (the western daimyo had already lost substantial resources through their support of the Korean Campaign).

The site selected for the castle was on the hill where the founder of Kyoto, Emperor Kammu, was buried. Hideyoshi had the Uji River dredged and diverted so it was possible to navigate from the castle to the Inland Sea via the Uji and Yodo rivers. Construction of the fortress required the services of between 20,000 and 30,000 men working day and night, who were furnished by the daimyo of more than 20 provinces. The rate of taxation for the project was rather steep—300 men per 10,000 koku of revenue. Building materials arrived from several areas, with necessary timbers originating in the Kiso district and floating down the rivers to the building site. Some buildings from Jurakudai were moved to Fushimi for use in the castle.[19]

When Hideyoshi died in 1598, Ieyasu took control and appointed his old friend Torii Mototada warden of the stronghold. By 1600, as we have seen in the section on Osaka Castle, the struggle for control of the country had begun to develop between Tokugawa and avid supporters of the House of Toyotomi. In May, the uprising began and Ieyasu started out from Osaka to put it down. On his way to Edo he stopped at Fushimi to visit with Torii and instructed him to hold the fortress to the last man. After he left, Shimazu Yoshihiro and Kobayakawa Hideake approached Torii and asked to join in the defense of the castle, but the latter doubted their loyalty and refused the offer. His suspicion was well founded, for on August 27 he discovered that his fortress of 1,800 men was surrounded by 40,000 men led by Kobayakawa, Shimazu, Ukita, and Nabeshima.[20] Since Fushimi was one of the newest strongholds, it was able to resist bombardment and assault so well that Torii passed the time playing *go* (a chess-like game). After some 10 days of stalemate, one of Kobayakawa's men set fire to the tower with a fire arrow, but it was quickly put out. Finally, on the morning of September 8, the fate of the defenders was sealed from within. One unit commander of the fortress and 40 men set fire to one of the courts, broke down 100 yards of wall, and made good their escape.[21]

In the confusion the attacking force crushed in the front gate and took several of the outer courts. The main keep was set ablaze, and at this point Torii was asked by some of his followers if they should commit suicide in the samurai tradition. Because his orders were to fight to the last man, he told them they must fight on, and he began to lead counterattacks with his 200 or so remaining men. The besiegers had now broken into the last defenses and were lying in ambush on either side of the gate to the main citadel. When the defenders ventured out in a headlong push against the enemy they were attacked from both sides. After three such forays Torii had 100 men left; after two more, he had only 10. As he sat down to rest on a step, one Saiga Shigetomo rushed up to him and was about to strike him down when he discovered his victim's identity. Saiga respectfully allowed Torii to disembowel himself before he took his head. Other defenders set fire to the bell tower and killed themselves, but at least one man escaped and reported the fate of Fushimi to Ieyasu. Almost all of the 1,800 defenders were killed in the battle, but the cost to the besiegers was some 3,000, making the victory of doubtful value to the Western Army.[22]

The fortress was rebuilt about 1602 by Ieyasu and made into an even stronger castle then before. In 1603 it was used in the ceremony that officially made the House of Tokugawa shogun of Japan. Until 1615 the castle was a place of some importance, but after the fall of the House of Toyotomi, the castle had begun to lose its prominence and parts of it were given away to various temples from time to time. The final dismantling was probably started in 1620, and, in 1623, some of the stone work was used to repair other castles. The main tower was moved to Nijo Castle in 1625, but it is likely this tower was not the lavish one originally built by Hideyoshi since that was reported to have been destroyed in the battle of 1600. Many of the castle's gates and structures were used to build shrines and temples in the Kyoto and Lake Biwa area, and the components may still be seen in these structures.

Today only a few walls and a moat of the original castle remain. A new donjon has been built, but there is a great deal of controversy about it. For one thing, it was not constructed on the site of the original keep, and since there is little or no information about the original appearance, the resemblance of the reconstructed model to the real one is a guess at best. Purists fear that the present structure was built solely for commercial purposes and not as a serious reproduction of what once existed.

◈ Nijo Castle

Nijo Castle, in the heart of Kyoto, was built in 1601[23] by Ieyasu on the site of the old Nijo Palace of Nobunaga's day (Fig. 25). It was more of a fortified residence than a full-sized castle, both in mass and arrangement. Its main purpose was to provide a place for the shogun to stay when he was in Kyoto and to serve as the headquarters of the *shoshidai* or governor of Kyoto under Tokugawa rule. The holder of this office, according to the Legacy of Ieyasu, had to be a fudai vassal and a general because he had the 33 western provinces under his control. The main duty of the shoshidai, however, was to act as a sort of jailer over the imperial court and its nobles to keep them from interfering in the real administration of the country.

Several significant events took place behind this castle's walls. Here Hideyori had his fateful interview with Ieyasu in 1611. Ieyasu also used the castle as a stopping place on his way to and from the Winter Campaign at Osaka Castle. In 1626 the emperor was invited to the castle by Iemitsu, Ieyasu's grandson, to help celebrate the completion of several structural additions. During this visit, lavish entertainment and gifts were given to the distinguished guests. In 1634 Iemitsu led a force of 300,000 men to Kyoto to impress the court with his power and to remind the daimyo in western Japan, most of whom were tozama, that the shogun was all-powerful. This was the last visit of any shogun to the court until the Restoration some 230 years later.

Enlargement and repair of the castle was made in 1625 and 1626 by Iemitsu and included the addition of the main tower which had been part of Fushimi Castle. The Kara Gate was also from Fushimi and is one of the remaining relics of that castle. During this period, Nijo was considerably expanded in its western section, and an inner compound with a surrounding moat was built. Iemitsu last used the castle in 1634, afterwards giving away many of the buildings. In 1663 an earthquake damaged the castle, and in 1791 the main tower was struck by lightning and destroyed.

In 1868 Emperor Meiji issued an edict from Nijo abolishing the shogunate and designating the palace the temporary seat of government, thus starting the Restoration of imperial rule. The palace at Nijo was appointed as a detached imperial palace and was used as Kyoto's prefectural office from 1871 until 1884 when it was taken over by the Imperial Household and used as an imperial summer palace (Fig. 26). During the time it was a public building the fine art work and craftsmanship of the building had been disgracefully defaced, and restoration of its splendor was undertaken in 1885–86. While this work was going on the hollyhock crest of the Tokugawa was removed and replaced by the 16-petaled chrysanthemum imperial crest whenever possible. In 1893 the residence of Prince Katsura was moved from the imperial palace grounds to the site of the donjon at Nijo. It was here that the enthronement banquet was held in 1928 for the present emperor. In 1939 the castle and its detached palace were given to the city of Kyoto.

The castle today covers about 70 acres and is surrounded by a moat and wall. It has two courts with gates on all sides of each court, and towers on the southeast and southwest corners of the secondary citadel, and by the east gate of the inner citadel on the south. The palace is approached through a court and entered through the *mi-kurumayose* or honorable carriage approach. From this point the visitor is conducted through five connected but separate buildings, the first of which consists of several chambers including one called the imperial messenger's chamber. The next building is entered from the first through a gallery and consists of three chambers; the middle chamber was used by the minister of the shogun when he was in Kyoto. This second building is called *shikidai*. The third building contains the *ohiroma* or great hall and four other chambers and was the audience hall of the shogun. The last chamber of this building is called the *sotetsu-no-ma* or Japanese fern-palm chamber. The next building is *kuroshoin* hall, which is somewhat smaller than the grand hall, but is beautifully decorated. The fifth building is the *shiroshoin* which contained the private apartments of the shogun with the nightingale boarding.

V

Important Historical Castles

◈ Odawara Castle

Odawara Castle was built at the dawn of feudalism in Japan (Fig. 27). The exact date is unknown, but it is believed that Minamoto Tomoasa erected a modest stronghold on a hill overlooking the Tokaido highway about 1180. The site was a strategic one because it guarded the approach to the vast Kanto plain and was the second line of defense, after the Hakone pass barrier, for the region from the west. The date when this castle was founded is also significant because the two great warrior houses, the Minamoto and the Taira, began their struggle for control of the country during this period. The first battle of this war (called the Gempei War) was fought about five miles south of the castle at Ishibashi-yama on September 14, 1180. Although the Minamoto forces lost the initial engagement and had to retire to the Hakone Mountains for regrouping, they eventually won the war in 1185. The son of Minamoto Tomoasa built a mansion called Hayakawa at the base of the small hill on which the castle stood. The site of this mansion was eventually incorporated into the rest of the castle as it expanded. Between the time of its founding and 1416, the stronghold passed through several families, but at the later date the Omori family took over the castle and held it for some 80 years.

Hojo Soun, who had his stronghold at Nirayama in the province of Izu, was to become the next lord of Odawara Castle.[1] This was the age of petty feudal barons who tried to expand their holdings by conquering neighboring territories. After analyzing the situation elsewhere, Soun decided that Odawara's location was the key to eventual control of the Kanto. He proceeded to make friends with the young Omori heir (who had recently succeeded his father), and obtained permission to hunt on Omori lands. Disguising his men as hunters, Soun led them on a hunt that ended in the massacre of the Omori and the capture of the strategic castle in 1495.[2] Soun as a result controlled Izu and southern Sagami provinces. Using his newly acquired stronghold as a base, he further expanded his territory and influence eastward. His design was to take over the area around Edo Bay, move northward in Musashi Province, and set up a line of defense to protect himself from invasion from the north. Between 1495 and 1518 he became the undisputed master of Sagami through a series of battles and sieges. Soun died at Nirayama in 1519 and his son, Ujitsuna, set out to finish the job his father had started. He nearly completed the task before his death in 1541. Ujitsuna's son, Ujiyasu, took over the family leadership and finally became the virtual master of the Kanto about 1560.

Prior to the Hojo takeover, Odawara had been nothing more than a post town along the Tokaido. As the influence and fame of the Hojo spread, the town grew in size attracting merchants, artisans, and tradesmen who heard of the need for their services by the daimyo and his retainers. Although the Hojo controlled the Kanto they were by no means completely secure from attack. Uesugi Kenshin made occasional raids on Hojo territory (he thought of himself as the legitimate ruler of the Kanto), and in 1560 he raided Odawara, blockading both the castle and the town. The siege did not last long because Kenshin was unable to provide a rear guard and was threatened by another old rival. After 1560 the situation settled down to the quiet tasks of everyday life. Peace did not prevail throughout Japan, however, for about this time Nobunaga and, after him, Hideyoshi were trying to unify the country by forcing the feudal lords of the west to submit to them. By 1587 Hideyoshi had taken control of western Japan —from Kyushu eastward to the approaches of the Kanto.

In 1589, as related in Chapter 2, he invited the fourth in the Hojo line, Ujimasa, to come to Kyoto and submit. Ujimasa, now in complete (or nearly complete) control of seven provinces, and sitting in a strongly fortified position at Odawara, felt he could resist any encroachment on his territory and refused to make the requested journey to court. He was determined to maintain the defensive attitude which seemed to work quite well in his dealings with lesser rivals. Unfortunately Ujimasa failed to realize that Hideyoshi was all-powerful in the west and had, in the course of just eight years, subdued all of the great warrior houses in the country. Hojo's neighbor, Ieyasu, made several attempts to get him to use reason and submit, but he only succeeded in getting Ujimasa's brother, Ujinori, to visit Hideyoshi.[3] Ujinori was in for several surprises when he arrived in Kyoto; for one thing he discovered that his style of clothing was several decades behind the times. For another he found that Hideyoshi had risen to the pinnacle of power. He was no longer just Nobunaga's stable boy who had made good and become a general, as the Hojo had fancied him. He was now *the* power in the country. Ujinori also discovered that his family was not considered to be of very high rank in court. Indeed, he found himself in a very low position—he was nothing more than a country squire in comparison to his counterparts from other parts of Japan.

After Ujinori made his court appearance, Hideyoshi visited him privately and emphasized how desirable it would be for the Hojo family to submit so they could take their proper place as equals with other feudal lords. Ujinori said that he would carry Hideyoshi's recommendation to his family, but if they did not accept it, he would not desert them but would do his best to defend their position. This made a favorable impression on Hideyoshi as an indication of Ujinori's character. When Ujinori returned to Odawara, he was unable to persuade his brother to come to terms. Hideyoshi then issued an ultimatum: submit or face annihilation.[4] At the same time Ujimasa was warned that hostilities would begin the following year and that his son, Ujinao, would surely lose his head as a result.

Even before this final demand was sent, Hideyoshi had started to prepare his move against the Hojo. He had his vassals send their families to Kyoto as hostages to guarantee their good behavior and began gathering and outfitting troops for the campaign. The assessments of the various daimyo were from four to seven men per 100 koku of revenue, with the heaviest dues, as already mentioned, assigned to Ieyasu.[5] The total number of men mustered for Hideyoshi was about 250,000. Of course Ujimasa had not been idle, and as early as the summer of 1587 had begun to assemble his army. The number of able-bodied men he had to draw from was limited, and he even had to take those who were in the service of shrines and monasteries. For the most part, the army consisted of warriors schooled in the older way of warfare with all too few of the type of professional, up-to-date soldier they were soon to face. Indeed, Ujimasa was hard pressed to gather 50,000 first-class fighting men.

Having assembled his army, Hideyoshi began to move his force toward the Hojo stronghold. Ieyasu advanced along the Tokaido while Sanada Masayuki took the Nakasendo (the central mountain road). About the same time a fleet of ships was sent out to patrol and blockade the Hojo coastline; some of them carried troops and supplies. The Hojo also had patrol boats off the Izu coast but they were no match for the muskets and cannon of the Western Fleet. Hideyoshi finally left the capital with great pomp on April 15, 1590, at the head of a force of some 170,000 men. After a leisurely trip up the Tokaido, they arrived at Numazu on May 1, and a short time later part of the force (about 40,000) lay siege to the castle at Nirayama, while the main force of about 150,000 moved on to Odawara, where they encircled the town as well as the castle. The besieging force also encamped on Ishigaki Hill northwest of the castle and performed a fete of psychological warfare. According to one story, a castle—or what appeared to be a castle from Odawara—was built there overnight. Actually, although there was a building (for it is said that some tens of thousands of men were put to work that night on it), the walls were made of paper.[6]

Meanwhile, Hojo Ujimasa had proposed to fight a decisive battle in the open, the winner take all. However, on the advice of one of his trusted advisors, it was decided to sit tight in the castle as Ujiyasu had done in 1560 when Uesugi Kenshin lay siege to it.

This counsel appeared to make sense because it was no doubt well known that the Hojo forces were considerably outnumbered, the castle was in a good defensive position, and it was well provided with arms and supplies.[7] The defenders were also sure that Hideyoshi would be unable to get sufficient, continuing supplies to carry out a long siege; they did not realize that he would be supplied by sea as well as by land. Short of betrayal by one of their own number, the Hojo forces felt they could hold out indefinitely.

The besiegers of Nirayama Castle vainly attempted to take it, but its 3,600-plus defenders not only withstood various storming methods, but ventured out from time to time to inflict sizable losses on the antagonists. It was not long, however, before all of the Hojo subsidiary fortresses, except Nirayama and Oshi, had fallen to Hideyoshi's forces, which had all but isolated the main citadel at Odawara.[8]

Hideyoshi was not one to advocate bloody warfare unnecessarily, and the well-defended castle convinced him that the best way to take the stronghold was to starve it out. He had decided to use this tactic before the campaign and had prepared for a long siege. To spare his men boredom and to keep them out of mischief, he allowed his commanders to build residences and tea rooms (all of which were landscaped), while his men planted gardens in which they grew such table items as melons and egg plant. Tradesmen from the western provinces were allowed to set up shop, selling everything from necessities to European imports. Innkeepers, restaurant operators, and women of loose morals also joined the party. Meanwhile, life within the castle walls was far from dull. The defenders were well supplied and passed the time playing *go*, drinking, and dancing, thus whiling away some 100 days of the siege.

The stand-off was not without skirmishes, including an instance when Ieyasu brought in miners to undermine part of the castle's defenses while other attackers broke in and set fire to some buildings. During this encounter the defenders inflicted some 300 casualties while suffering 400 of their own. In spite of this and several similar operations, however, the besieging forces only succeeded in destroying a few towers and sections of wall.

For the most part, indeed, the opposing forces were courteous

FIG. 23. Such steps and stone walls as these are almost all that remain of the once magnificent Azuchi Castle.

Fig. 24. Rebuilt tenshu-kaku or keep of Osaka Castle.

FIG. 25. Corner tower and front gate of Nijo Castle.

FIG. 28. Double bridge leading to the nishi-maru, and a corner turret (Edo Castle).

FIG. 29. Genkan or entry porch of a daimyo's mansion (Kanazawa Castle).

FIG. 30. A reconstruction of the original keep. The secondary keep is barely visable on the right (Kumamoto Castle).

and considerate of each other. Some of Hideyoshi's commanders approached Ujimasa several times to urge him to capitulate, each time sending along a keg of good liquor to "cheer" him. Ujimasa returned the favor by presenting them with bullets and powder. One Kuroda Josui visited the Hojos and received a sword and a conch which were said to be two treasures of the Hojo House. The battle itself was a standstill, prompting Hideyoshi to make one last effort to effect a surrender by offering to confirm Ujimasa in the provinces of Izu and Sagami. The offer was refused.

Ujimasa little suspected that before the siege had begun, Hideyoshi had bought off Ujimasa's most trusted advisor, Matsuda Norihide (the one who had advised Ujimasa against warfare in the open). As the siege wore on, Matsuda contacted the besieging force and made arrangements secretly to admit the assailants to the castle. Matsuda had tried to get his sons to join the plot, but they refused. One of them reported his father's treachery to Ujimasa, on the condition that the traitor would not be put to death. But when the truth was known, all promises were cast aside and Matsuda was slain.

Following the plot's exposure, suspicion and mistrust began to permeate the defending forces, and some of the commanders wanted to desert. Although there are several versions of the capitulation, the main points are basically the same.[9] Ujimasa's sons, Ujinao and Ujifusa (Ieyasu's son-in-law), met with Ieyasu to arrange the surrender of the castle. Ujinao proposed that he be allowed to commit suicide and that the rest of the defenders be left unharmed; this offer was turned down by Hideyoshi. Finally, on August 6, the castle was surrendered and Ieyasu took possession of it. Ujimasa and his brothers, Ujiteru and Ujinori (the defender of Nirayama), were taken to the home of Tamara, a physician, to await their fate. Two days later the decision was handed down by Hideyoshi and Ieyasu—Ujimasa, Ujiteru, and their two chief counselors were to commit *seppuku*. The two brothers bathed, as was the custom, and then disemboweled themselves after which Ujinori cut off their heads;[10] he was about to turn the sword on himself, but was prevented from taking his own life. The sons of Ujimasa were sent to a monastery on Mount Koya, and later Ujinao was given a small fief in Kawachi with a revenue of

10,000 koku; he died there of smallpox a year later at the age of 21.[11] Ujinori made a very favorable impression on Hideyoshi (it will be remembered that he was on good terms with Ieyasu), and he was awarded a fief of 3,000 koku in Kawachi and later received another of 10,000 at Sayama.

After Odawara, the whole of Kanto fell into Hideyoshi's hands, and its eight provinces were given to Ieyasu in exchange for his holdings in Mikawa. Another result of the campaign, as already mentioned, was that the barons to the north (such as Date) submitted to Hideyoshi, thus completing the task of unifying the country.

Under the Tokugawas, Odawara Castle had several masters. Okubo Tadachika was lord of the fief during the early 17th century but, for some unknown reason, he took up the unhealthy habit of disobeying shogunate regulations. He failed to attend court in Edo *(sankin kotai)* for a period of three years, dug a moat around part of the castle without first obtaining permission, and arranged the marriage of his son without getting approval from Edo—all in direct violation of feudal regulations. By 1613 the shogunate apparently had had enough of Okubo, and it ordered him to Kyoto to oversee an inquisition against the Christians there. While he was gone, Ieyasu, his son Hidetada, and their counselors went to Odawara and declared that since a marriage had been arranged without permission, Tadachika's son would be dispossessed of the fief. The castle was ordered dismantled immediately, and local people began the task with the assistance of a large host from Edo who had come for that purpose. In a relatively short time, the gates, walls, and other defenses were torn down.

After the dismantling, the castle was left unoccupied until 1619 when the Abe family became its master for about five years. It was again vacant from 1625 to 1632 when the Inaha family became lord of the fief and ruled over it for three generations. In 1685 the descendants of the Okubo family were awarded the fief, and they occupied the castle for ten generations until the close of the Edo period in 1868. The following year it was returned to the emperor as part of the Restoration of Imperial Power, and it was ordered dismantled in 1870. All that remained standing at this time were the corner turrets, superstructure of the donjon, stone walls, and moat. Besides the destruction suffered at the hands of men, earthquakes also took their toll. During the Edo period alone, there were at least six recorded tremblers that caused considerable damage.[12] After each, repairs were made to a greater or lesser degree.

At the height of its greatness, Odawara Castle boasted an inner court that was 130 yards by 145 yards, a second court of over 700 square yards, and a third court that encompassed the other two. It had an outer defense wall that was almost a mile long and varied in height from 18 to 35 feet.[13] The fortress also had 14 turrets, 5 bridges, 26 gates, and 6 inner gardens. During feudal days the castle occupied a commanding position along the Tokaido and was the ninth station (of 53) along this main road between Edo and Kyoto.

The reconstructed donjon, built in 1960, is made of reinforced concrete and is designed like models of the original. It is some 125 feet high, including a 35-foot stone base; it has two copper dolphins on the roof, each $6\frac{1}{2}$ feet tall and weighing 906 pounds. The tower has four stories and three sets of eaves. On the first floor is a display of local products, the second and third floors are used as a museum and art gallery, and the fourth floor has an outlook platform. A zoo occupies the old inner court. Part of the moat, several turrets and bridges, and portions of the walls remain today.

◆ Edo Castle

The most magnificent castle in all of Japan was at Edo. It was here that the Tokugawa shogunate set up its headquarters and established the administrative capital of the country early in the 17th century.[14] It is sometimes called Chiyoda Castle, that being the name of a village that once stood on the castle site (Fig. 28).

Edo was founded in 1465 by Ota Dokan, who, along with his father, Koshin, was known as a castle builder. As a chief retainer of Uesugi Sadamasa, governor of the area under the Ashikaga shogunate, Dokan was charged with the responsibility of defending Kamakura from attack from the east. To this end, he established strongholds at Kawagoe and Iwatsuki in Musashi Province in addition to the one he occupied near present-day Shinagawa in Tokyo. Besides these strongholds, he also built a chain of lookout stations in the area. One of these was located in a place called Kato, ideal as a strong defensive position because of its commanding view of the surrounding territory and its site at a point where several rivers flowed into Edo Bay. These waterways gave good communications to the interior of the wide, reedy Musashi plain. It was here that Dokan decided to build his chief defensive position and make his home.

In laying out the castle, Dokan found that three villages, Chiyoda, Takurata, and Iwaita, were within its confines. The general line of the defense in the event of attack from the east was to stop the invaders at the Tone River. Should the defenders fail at this point, they would fall back to the castle and make their stand there. A description of the castle given in a book entitled *Kotei-ki*, written in 1476, states that the ramparts were steep and over 100 feet high, and the walls were built of stone. The castle had deep ditches and wide moats filled with water bridged by large timbers. The interior was guarded by iron gates and stone barricades, and passageways were paved with stone. Inside the castle compound there were towers, the residence of the daimyo, godowns, barracks, and stables.[15] Although the castle was remarkable for its day, it in fact probably resembled a Roman camp, with its deep, wide ditch, high walls topped with a palisade, and heavy wooden doors at the gates.

Dokan was murdered in 1485 on Sadamasa's command because a rival of Dokan's spread a false rumor about his loyalty. Possession of the stronghold was then given to Soga Bungo, another of Sadamasa's retainers. Later it was transferred to the lord's two sons, Tomoyoshi and Tomooki, the latter being forced to abandon the castle when it was besieged by Hojo Ujitsuna of Odawara in 1524. The Toyama and Tominaga families, retainers of the Hojo, held the area for the Hojo until 1590 when the family was defeated by Hideyoshi at Odawara. It was during the siege of the latter castle that Hideyoshi offered Ieyasu the eight Kanto provinces in exchange for his holdings west of the Hakone Barrier. The offer was accepted, and Ieyasu entered the castle September 1, 1590.

When he arrived at Edo, Ieyasu found the castle in a mess. The steps were made of old ships' boards, and the enclosures were small and unsightly; buildings were dilapidated because no repairs had been made after Hojo's siege. Rain had leaked in through the cedar plank and thatched roof and had stained the floor mats. The defenses consisted of wide, dry ditches and grass-covered embankments, none of which were faced with stone. There were three enclosures, the chief one standing on a hill and the other two below, all separated from one another by dry moats. The site of the future west court was on hilly ground overgrown with fruit trees.[16] The only immediate repairs Ieyasu made were to plug up the leaks, renew some of the floor mats, and fill in the inner moat.

The surrounding area was desolate. On the land side there was a wilderness of reeds on the low ground where the Sumida River and other streams made their way through marshes on their way to the sea. Quantities of bamboo grass grew on the higher ground; the area where some of the most valuable land in Tokyo now stands (Nihonbashi district) was under sea water; and the present day Hibiya area was a beach where fishermen had their huts. It is no wonder then that Ieyasu's retainers were bewildered at the choice of this place for his capital instead of Odawara, which had everything a feudal lord and his retainers could want. But he had made up his mind to establish at Edo, and he went about awarding fiefs to his retainers and building some 30 fortresses around his capital at distances of 10 to 50 miles out. Most of these were awarded to fudai daimyo, the hereditary Tokugawa vassals.

Between 1593 and 1636 the castle was expanded and improved until it became undisputably the largest and most majestic castle in the country. Although building was carried on throughout this time, the major changes were made during the decade beginning in 1604 (the year after Ieyasu was made shogun). It was then that the city of Edo was laid out and constructed. The object was not only to build a capital and castle fitting for the shogun but also to reduce the wealth of the daimyo by making them supply labor, materials, and money for the construction (a frequently used tactic, as we have seen), thereby lessening their ability to overthrow the Tokugawa dynasty. To this end, some of the daimyo were called upon to supply the large stones needed to face the ramparts and moats. These stones came mostly from Izu and were transported by ships to Edo, the 3,000 ships required being provided by other daimyo. For each 100,000 koku of income, the daimyo were to furnish 1,120 stones of a size that took 100 men each to handle. Each ship was to carry two of these huge stones and to make two trips to Izu a month. In addition to the job of facing the moats, other moats were dug during this period—altogether an expensive and time-consuming operation.

At the same time it was decided to reclaim some of the land on the sea side of the castle so it could be used for the expanding city. In order to obtain fill for this project, Kanda Hill was leveled, and the dirt was moved to the reclamation site. The two-square-mile area thus formed is now the main business section of Tokyo. This enormous task was carried out by ten daimyo who had to supply one man for each 1,000 koku of revenue. It is estimated that there were at least 10,000 men working on this phase of building. Although the land reclaimed could not be considered choice property for home building, it was good enough for the townspeople. Of course, the outcome of this project forever changed the geography of the area, for now Edo was a plain from Shinagawa to Kudan Hill in one direction and Asakusa in the other.

In 1606 work was begun again on the castle after a few months of rest. This time the keep was started, and the main court was built. The main palace and ramparts were also completed as well as the second and third courts and stone walls of the outer defenses. It is said that there were some 300,000 workers employed during this phase of building. The work was completed during the same year, and the daimyo were excused and allowed to return to their domains. All of the construction up to that point had been performed by the daimyo from western Japan.

When work was resumed the following year, lords of the east and north were called upon to do their part. The daimyo from the Kanto region provided 180 square feet of stone per 1,000 koku of revenue (800,000 koku was involved) for construction, and they also completed the main keep. At the same time many of the 120-foot-wide ramparts were increased in height by 12 feet, raising them to 60 feet. The outer wall was also increased in height from 12 to 40 feet and a moat was dug; in 1611 additional moats and ramparts were built. In 1612 and 1613 the provincial lords were again called upon to supply materials and labor to finish the fortifications. In addition to other projects completed at this time, the moated enclosure in front of the west court between the Sakurada and Ote Gates was constructed for use as a residential site for the more important daimyo. Work was finally completed in 1614 much to the relief of the contributing daimyo. During the construction the shogun Hidetada made daily inspection tours to view the progress. Apparently this was quite fatiguing, for tea rooms were conveniently located around the project for his refreshment.

In 1636 an outer moat was dug that ran from the Suidobashi area to the sea. Filled with water from the Kanda River, this moat was enlarged between 1658 and 1661 by the Lord of Sendai so it would be a navigable link between the bay and the river. In return for doing this work, the retainers of the daimyo had the privilege of passing through the Asakusa Gate with slow matches attached to their matchlocks when coming or going to their castle town.

In 1600 Ieyasu had decided to make Edo his capital, and by 1609 the population of the town had reached about 150,000, according to Rodrigo de Vivero y Velasco, the Spanish governor of the Philippines (1608–9). In 1602 Ieyasu established a library in the city and obtained many books for it from an old library at Kanazawa.

When the construction was finally completed, the castle consisted of the chief enclosure (hon-maru), western enclosure (nishi-maru) where the retired shogun and the heir apparent to the shogunate resided, and second and third enclosures (ni-no-maru and san-no-maru). Each of these courts was separated from the others by high walls and moats that made them individual castles within the larger plan. Inside the chief enclosure was the palace of the shogun. It was a one-story affair, but was higher than most buildings. The interior was arranged in three major divisions: (1) the great outer palace or *o-omote,* which contained reception rooms for public audience and apartments for guards and some officials;

(2) middle interior or *naka-oku,* where the shogun met with his relatives, more important lords, and carried on the affairs of state with his counselors; and (3) great interior or *o-oku,* which contained the apartments of the shogun and his ladies-in-waiting. Few men were allowed to enter this innermost portion of the palace, and messages to and from it were carried by young boys. The grand audience hall was said to be 1,000 mats in size and could be closed off and made into many smaller rooms by use of sliding screen partitions covered with fine paper on which elegant designs were drawn.

Immediately behind the o-oku palace was the great donjon that towered five stories above the city. Behind the western enclosure lay Fukiage park, which gave the castle inhabitants a touch of the country while living in the center of a large city. The chief enclosure, besides containing the shogun's palace and great keep, also housed the treasury. This consisted of three storehouses that bordered on a rampart in the back and on a semicircular stone wall adjoining the palace on the other side. The only entrance to the compound was through a small gateway made of heavy timbers. From the wall at the back there was a sheer 60-foot drop to the moat below. Thus situated, the treasury was the most secure area in the castle.

Francois Caron, a director of the Dutch factory at Deshima, told of the castle being surrounded by three deep moats and counterscape. The moats in turn were bordered by stone walls. He also remarked that it was difficult to get a general idea of the castle plan because the courts led from one to another in such a manner as to confuse the outsider. He described the streets within the castle as being very large and having the *yashiki* (mansions) of the daimyo built on either side. The park contained ponds, gardens, rivers, and woods, and there were places for sports and the training of troops.

Rodrigo de Vivero y Velasco, who also visited Japan at this time, saw 20,000 servants between the first gate and the shogun's chamber. He marveled at the huge stones that made up the walls, the latter constructed without mortar. There were openings in the walls through which artillery could be fired (but there did not seem to be a great deal of it). As he went into the castle, he crossed over a moat on the largest drawbridge he had ever seen. Entering the gate, he passed through two ranks of 1,000 soldiers who were armed with muskets and matchlocks. After walking 100 paces to the second gate, he was escorted by 400 men armed with pikes and lances to the third gate. Upon passing through this he saw the stables which had room for more than 200 horses and an armory that contained enough weapons for 100,000 men.

When Edo Castle was developed to its fullest, it had 38 gates guarding it. Over the years most of these have been destroyed by fire and earthquake, including the 1923 earthquake that destroyed the only gates surviving to modern times. The main gate, the ote-mon, had a guard of 120 men, while those further in the depths of the castle had a guard of between 30 and 70. Caron noted that the gates were not placed in a straight line, but were staggered so a person seeking passage had to go in a half circle to find the next one. The actual circumference of the castle compound is open to debate. Caron said that it was six English miles, but other authorities maintain that it was more like ten miles around (Fig. 31).

Inside the outer Sakurada Gate stood the houses of the daimyo, but some of the more important daimyo and various important shogunate officials had their residences within the inner moat. At first Ieyasu did not care to have these lords living in Edo, but even before Sekigahara some of them sent their families and the families of their chief retainers to the city as voluntary hostages to demonstrate their loyalty. After the decisive struggle, almost all of the daimyo prevailed upon the shogunate to grant them land on which to build mansions in the city. The officials finally gave in and designated land for the purpose outside the outer Sakurada Gate, which was then uneven ground covered with brambles and many low spots. This land was eventually made usable for building sites when earth from excavation of the moats was brought in and used for fill. Most of the mansions were situated southeast and east of the castle inside the outer moat, but some daimyo received building sites southwest of the castle just outside the inner moat. In general these houses were located so they were handy to the castle for the convenience of the daimyo who had to take their turns on duty at the shogun's court.

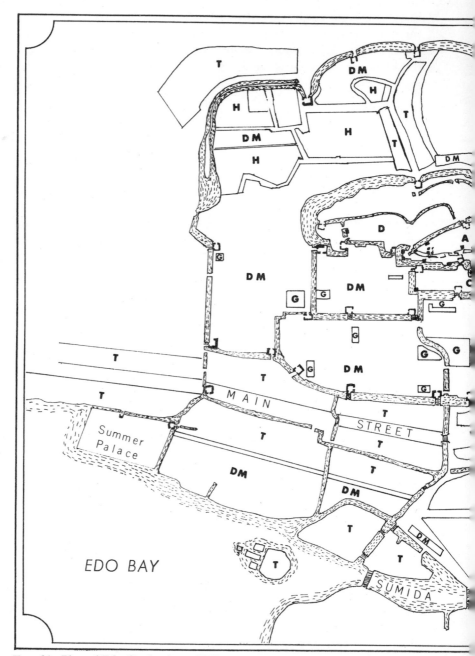

FIG. 31. Plan of Edo Castle about 1850.

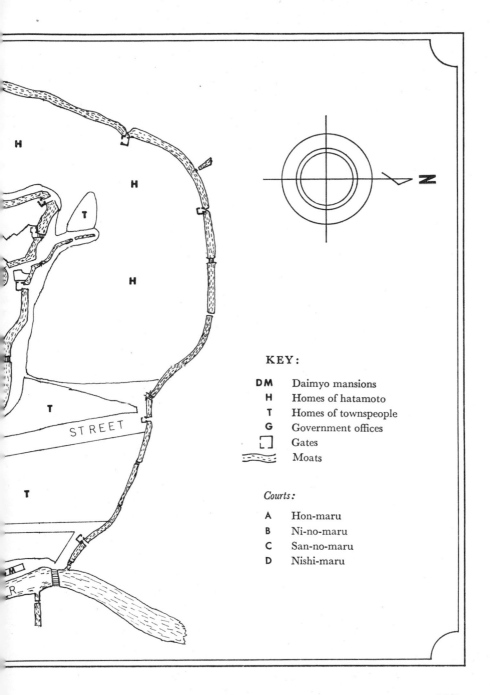

KEY:

DM	Daimyo mansions
H	Homes of hatamoto
T	Homes of townspeople
G	Government offices
⌑	Gates
〰	Moats

Courts:

A	Hon-maru
B	Ni-no-maru
C	San-no-maru
D	Nishi-maru

These mansions were most elaborate. They were built in rectangular blocks with four to six in each block and were so arranged that no more than two sides of the enclosure faced a street. Between the street and the mansion's outer buildings was a stone-faced ditch, usually three to eight feet wide (although some were as wide as 15 feet), used mostly for drainage. A causeway bridged these ditches from the street to the gates. Each mansion had several gates used for various purposes, designed according to fairly strict regulations depending on the importance of the owner. The number of gates allowed was also based upon the same criterion. The main gate was a double opening supported by heavy iron-plated beams; the gate was held closed by a beam that rested in iron sockets. The main gates at mansions of the more important daimyo had porter's lodges in them. The gates usually were part of the outer wall, but sometimes they were separate structures. There were also smaller gates that were of the sliding variety fastened from within and were used primarily for emergency.

The outer-most structure of the mansion was the *nagaya,* a long, narrow building that formed the outer wall of the grounds and served as barracks for the daimyo's retainers. The roof was tiled and the rectangular windows were barred. Those belonging to larger mansions generally were two-stories high, while those of the smaller ones were one story. The roofs were supported by large beams, and the walls between them were made from planks that were plastered on the upper third and painted black on the lower two thirds. Walls that were not a nagaya were made of mud and plaster, had tiled roofs, and were six to ten feet high. The inner side of the nagaya had sliding doors that gave entry to the rooms within; they were square and had one window. At the larger houses five retainers shared a room on the upper floor, and their servents had quarters on the ground floor. The nagaya was screened from the rest of the mansion proper by a fence a short distance from the structure.

Within the main gate was a courtyard, the size and paving depending upon the rank of the owner—the more important the daimyo, the larger his courtyard. The paving ranged from the whole area covered with flagstone, to part of it paved and the rest covered with large pebbles, to a bare yard with only a paved path leading to the main hall at the more modest mansions. Sometimes the visitor was confronted with a stone-faced wall and a mazelike approach to the main hall, which was similar to the approach one finds at some castles.

Between the nagaya and the main hall stood the homes and offices of the clan officials. The houses were ordinary, one-story Japanese style with a large entry porch. They were called *naka-nagaya* or inner-barracks. Each one was surrounded by a fence, shrubbery, or a wall, which made the inner area a series of smaller compounds. The size of the buildings and compounds was dictated by the amount of space available (which in turn was dictated by the rank of the daimyo). Occasionally clan officials were housed in the nagaya. Also within this area were various fireproof stone-houses.

In the center of the grounds was the main hall or residence of the daimyo. It was surrounded by a plastered wall or a plank screen, and the paved surface described above led directly to the *genkan* or entry porch of this building (Fig. 29). Inside the genkan was a reception table manned by attendants who received guests and ushered them to the inner waiting chambers called *sho-in*. Behind the chambers were the quarters of the occupants and, usually at the extreme rear of the building, a wide, lofty, main audience hall with a raised dais.

The grounds of the mansion were usually beautifully landscaped, complete with waterfalls, pools, trees, and shrubs. Many were quite elaborate, at least two of them having had models of the 53 post towns of the Tokaido.

In addition to having the *kami* or chief yashiki or mansion, many daimyo also kept one or two others located at a distance from the castle. These were called *naka* or middle and *shimo* or lower yashiki. In addition, some daimyo had a *besso* or summer residence which was smaller than the yashiki and had more charming gardens and lighter defenses than did the larger mansion.

The shogun's lesser vassals were granted building sites for more modest homes to the north and west of the castle in an area sometimes called the *bancho*. This was on hilly ground, but the authorities had it leveled enough so the houses could be built without these lesser retainers going to added expense. This area was chosen because of its close proximity to the castle, where the retainers served as guards. In 1689 land was granted to vassals who held certain official appointments east of the Sumida River in the Honjo district. The grants of land, between 6,400 and 18,000 square feet, were a little larger than those closer to the castle.

To the east and south of the castle lay the section set aside for merchants, but much of this area was not suitable for building because it was marshy land. Dirt excavated from the moats was piled in the area, and the merchants were allowed to haul it away for use as fill. Thus was formed the land that today is so valuable. All merchants or artisans in the same trade had their places of business on the same street which was named after that trade, for example, lumber street, tub-maker's street, and so forth.

No description of Edo would be complete without mention of Yoshiwara, the gay quarter of the city, for it was here that the brothels and restaurants were found. It had been reclaimed from a reedy area by using fill dirt in much the same manner as that used by the merchants, and was enclosed by a wall that had only one entrance so the local police could observe the comings and goings of the district's patrons and constantly watch for criminals who were attracted there. Within the walls of Yoshiwara was a city within a city, complete with merchants who catered exclusively to the district's inhabitants and their customers. Although the district suffered several fires during its history and was moved from time to time as a result, it generally remained in the area of Asakusa in modern-day Tokyo.

In 1636 Edo was officially made the administrative capital of Japan, and about this time it became mandatory for all daimyo to observe sankin kotai, the system, mentioned previously, that the shogunate instituted to attain absolute control over the feudal lords.[17] As a result of becoming the capital of the country, Edo also became a large commercial and cultural center.

The city and its castle suffered many natural catastrophes. In 1647 an earthquake damaged the castle and mansions of many of the daimyo. The worst disaster of this early period occurred 10 years later when a three-day fire swept the city. Known as the Great Fire of Meireki, it was fanned by a gale-force northwest wind and was fed by drought-dried wooden structures. The wind shifted on the evening of the second day, driving the flames toward the center of the city from the southern section, and upon reaching Kojimachi, it destroyed the houses of servants and retainers of the daimyo. It was at this point that the castle itself was set ablaze, fire destroying the outer courts and damaging the keep. All of the mansions near the castle were completely gutted. The final toll amounted to destruction of more than half the city and an estimated 100,000 killed.

Rebuilding started immediately and was finished in about two years. The city was better planned, and particular attention was given to the area devoted to wholesale trade. The needs of townspeople were also adequately cared for with the shogunate providing them with food until they were re-established. Money was advanced for constructing shops and homes. Funds were also lent to the daimyo for rebuilding their mansions. Repairs to the castle and palace of the shogun were the last major projects undertaken before the shogun returned to his headquarters within the castle walls in 1659.

Other disasters followed. In 1703 a great earthquake destroyed a large part of the city including several daimyo mansions and damaged some of the castle walls. There was also much loss of life as a result of this event. In 1707 Mt. Fuji erupted causing earthquakes and covering a large area with ashes. Fortunately there was little loss of life during the conflagration. Another large fire, almost as great as the Meireki fire, struck Edo in 1772. At that time four gates of the castle were destroyed.

We have seen that the population of Edo reached about 150,000 by 1609; by 1693 it was 350,000 and 500,000 by 1700. About 30 years later the population was set at 561,900 excluding the shogun's retainers and those of the daimyo. By 1787 the figure had reached 1,367,900, making Edo one of the world's largest cities at that time.

The fortunes of the shogunate began to fade rapidly toward the middle of the 19th century. It lost control over the tozama daimyo, who no longer were required to abide by the alternate residence regulations and now stayed in their fiefs. In some cases they were even in open revolt against the shogun. Inability to control their vassals was a sign of shogunate weakness in the eyes of anti-shogunate elements, and this conclusion was further strengthened when it appeared the shogun had been forced to come to terms with the Americans, Perry and Harris. After a brief civil war, the shogunate was defeated by pro-imperial elements led by the Choshu and Satsuma Clans, and by early 1868 the entire country had submitted to the emperor. Shortly thereafter, the imperial court moved from the ancient capital of Kyoto to the shogun's castle in Edo. At the same time the name of the city was changed to Tokyo or Eastern Capital.

During this period of political change the castle at Edo was undergoing changes, too, but these were made by fire. Between 1844 and 1863 the chief enclosure was burned three times. When this happened the shogun usually moved to the western enclosure, but in 1853 both of these were destroyed at about the same time, and the shogun was forced to move in with some of the daimyo. On May 5, 1873 the western enclosure burned for the last time and was never rebuilt.

After the Restoration, Tokyo underwent rapid modernization, although reminders of feudal days remained, such as the winding and bending streets. On September 1, 1923 at 11:58 A.M. disaster struck the city again. An earthquake, centered about 60 miles to the south, shook the east coast of central Honshu, causing much damage and loss of life. In Tokyo a large number of structures were demolished or severely damaged. More than 100 fires spread and burned about half of the city in three days. Many of the castle gates were destroyed, but were later rebuilt of reinforced concrete and may be seen today.[18]

During the bombing and fire raids of the Pacific War in 1945 the castle escaped with little damage although much of the city and the palace were reduced to ashes. It was in the early morning hours of August 10, 1945 in an air-raid shelter beneath the palace grounds that the emperor made the decision to accept the Potsdam Declaration and end the war. Today a large part of the outer moat remains along with the gates reconstructed after the 1923 earthquake, the walls, and the turrets. In October 1968 the inner, second, and third courts of the castle were opened to the public, and the visitor may now see the foundation of the once-mighty keep and the inner castle grounds.

◆ Mito Castle

Very little is still extant of what was once Mito Castle, a castle that played a significant part in Japanese history for two reasons. First, it was the seat of government for Mito Province and was one of the *sanke* or "three houses" of the Tokugawa family.[19] The lord of this province also had the hereditary position of vice shogun and was thereby prohibited from becoming shogun.

The other historical point of importance is that Mito was the base of political thinking in Japan. The second lord of the province, Mitsukuni, Ieyasu's grandson, started compiling the *Dai Nihon Shi* or *Great History of Japan* in 1657. This monumental work was not completed until 1906 (perhaps because some of Mitsukuni's descendants were not as zealous about the task as he). In its final form the study comprises some 397 volumes and 20,964 pages. An important theme is that the legitimate ruler of Japan is the emperor, and that the shogun was acting as his loyal minister.

As other intellectuals read this work during the first part of the 19th century, they began to see that the emperor was a prisoner of the shogun. Widespread economic difficulties, combined with the shogun's opening of the country to foreigners, led these thinkers to plot rebellion. The anti-shogunate movement was encouraged by teachers in various parts of the country, notably those at Mito and at Choshu in western Honshu.

The last lord of Mito, Yoshinobu, became shogun in 1866 in spite of the prohibition against a member of the Mito branch attaining the position. In 1868 he resigned as shogun and handed over his power, rank, and lands to the emperor. Daimyo loyal to the throne also surrendered their holdings and took up arms against those forces that opposed the changeover.

Of Mito Castle, only earthworks and part of the moat remain. A donjon once stood in the first ring of the fortification rather than in the inner-most citadel as is typical of castles. In some respects it resembled an old-time Japanese storehouse because it had thick white-plastered walls. Most of the buildings were destroyed by fire during the hostilities of the Restoration, and the few remaining were demolished by air raids in 1945.

◈ Kumamoto Castle

On Chausuyama, overlooking the city of Kumamoto, stands the castle built by Kato Kiyomasa between 1601 and 1607 (Fig. 30). The hill had been used as a castle site as early as the second quarter of the 16th century, but it was a minor fortification until the castle was thoroughly remodeled. Kato is renowned in history as a castle architect, and his castle at Kumamoto, with its high stone walls and deep moats, is a good example of his skill. It was ranked with the great castles of Osaka and Nagoya as one of Japan's finest.

In its prime the castle covered an area of about one mile east to west and $2\frac{1}{4}$ miles north to south, while its outer moat measured over $5\frac{1}{2}$ miles in circumference. The defenses within the moat included 49 turrets, 18 turret gates, and 29 other gates. In the main citadel were two donjons, the principal one six stories high with three sets of eaves and a basement. Its unique feature was a first floor built on beams that overhung the stone base and protruded over the moat. During battle, the floor boards could be removed, and projectiles such as rocks could be dropped on would-be invaders. The secondary keep was connected to the first, but was somewhat smaller, with only four stories and two sets of eaves. It was about 67 feet high. Both of these keeps were plastered with mud, covered with wood, and painted black. The Udo turret, which is about the only building remaining of the original castle, has often been referred to as the third donjon. It is well preserved and gives one an excellent idea of how the other donjons were built. This turret consists of a basement, five floors, and three sets of eaves. The lines of the roofs are straight and do not curve upward as is usual in castle design.

Kato Kiyomasa died in 1611 and his son, Tadahiro, became lord of the fief. Tadahiro fell into disgrace with the shogunate in 1632 and was exiled to northern Honshu. Hosokawa Tadaoki, lord of Kokura Castle, was given the fief the same year, and his descendants remained in possession until the end of the feudal period.[20] When Tadaoki moved to Kumamoto from Kokura, he retired in favor of his son, Tadatoshi.

The remainder of the feudal period was uneventful in the fief, and the inmates of Kumamoto appear to have been little involved in the events that occurred in neighboring areas. In 1637–38 the Shimabara Revolt took place just across the bay from Kumamoto on the Shimabara Peninsula where some 37,000 peasants and ronin lost their lives at Hara Castle. And later, the daimyo of Satsuma Province, adjacent to Kumamoto, was very active in the Restoration movement, but the people of the Kumamoto fief played no part in this historical event.

Kumamoto Castle was the scene of unrest, however, during the Satsuma Rebellion of 1877. This uprising resulted from discontent among former samurai who had lost their stipends of rice and were left with little means of support. The rebellion of 1877 was the culmination of a chain of events that began in October 1873 when Saigo Takamori, who stood for the traditional loyalties to his home province of Satsuma and the samurai cause, resigned his position as commander of the Imperial Guard in Tokyo. The cause of his resignation was the governmental rejection of his plan to invade Korea and thereby give the hard-pressed samurai employment. Saigo retired to Kagoshima and set up a private school at which he trained samurai in traditional military skills. The number of his students grew to 20,000, and his influence increased proportionately. Before long the imperial government could make no move in the area without his tacit approval. Because of a series of governmental actions that further weakened the cause of the samurai, Saigo's followers became restless, prompting the government to order removal of a store of arms at Kagoshima. Word of this move leaked out, and the malcontents, claiming that they had uncovered a plot to assassinate Saigo, raided the stores before they could be moved.

Saigo's followers were now getting out of hand, and in order to control them, Saigo agreed to lead them to Tokyo where he proposed to restate his demand for an invasion of Korea. As a result of this action, he was declared a rebel on February 20, 1877, and a subjugation army was formed to put down the insurrection. What Saigo had hoped would be a triumphal march to Tokyo ended rather abruptly at Kumamoto when he met stubborn resistance from the government garrison stationed at the castle. On February 22 his 15,000-man army lay siege to the fortress, and for nearly two months the two forces exchanged fire and eventually destroyed the castle. While the siege was on, representatives of the government landed in Kagoshima and persuaded the residents to remain loyal to the emperor. Supporting units of Saigo's army in the city were captured, and the besieged force at Kumamoto was relieved on April 15. The rebels then retreated to Kagoshima.

There were skirmishes all over southern Kyushu as rebels were pursued southward until the final battle was fought on the slopes of Mount Shiroyama near Kagoshima. What was left of Saigo's army dug in on the mountain and was faced with seven battalions of imperial troops and a corps of police. In a final sweep up the mountain, the loyal forces brought the rebellion to an end.[21] After this, Kumamoto Castle continued to be used as a garrison, and, according to *Murry's Handbook* of 1913, permission still had to be obtained to visit the castle ruins.

Kumamoto was without a castle donjon until 1960 when a reinforced concrete replica of the original keep was built at a cost of some $500,000. Since the original foundation, which remained after the battle, could not possibly support the 6,500-ton structure, it was necessary to build the main keep on eight piles, $6\frac{1}{2}$ feet in diameter, driven 144 feet into the ground; the secondary keep required four piles. The new keeps appear to be suspended in mid-air because the piling is about a foot above the original foundation. Within the original base of the main tower remain the old well and a set of steps that once led to the first floor. From the observation deck 260 feet above sea level, a panoramic view of the surrounding area, from Mount Aso to Ariake Bay, can be seen.

VI

Castles of Interest

◆ Gifu Castle

Gifu, as noted before, was a fortified site early in Japan's feudal history. A castle was first built on Inaba Hill in 1201, but it was later abandoned. Restored in the 15th century, it was the stronghold of Saito Dosan in the middle of the 16th century. He was killed by his son in 1566, and this son then offered strong resistance to Nobunaga when he attempted to take over the area. In 1567 Nobunaga's forces succeeded in storming the castle; it was in this year that the castle was destroyed by fire (whether as a result of battle or a mishap is unknown), but it was rebuilt by Nobunaga. A place of splendor, judging from the description by Father Frois,[1] it was later occupied by Nobunaga's son and grandson.

Some sources say that the castle was abandoned again in 1590 and the buildings torn down at that time. However, it is known that Ishida Mitsunari went to Gifu after he destroyed Fushimi Castle and was warmly welcomed by Oda Hidenobu. Shortly thereafter the castle was taken by elements of Ieyasu's forces on the eve of the battle at Sekigahara. After this, the domain that had been Gifu's was placed under the control of the Owari Clan with headquarters at Nagoya.

A replica of the castle was built atop Inaba Hill in 1910, but this structure was destroyed during the Pacific War. The present three-story keep was built in 1956.

◈ Ogaki Castle

Founded in 1535, Ogaki Castle was expanded and modified over the years (Fig. 32). In 1596 a four-story keep was built within its precincts, and it is this tower that makes the castle unique among those of Japan because the words "four" and "death" are pronounced the same in Japanese, a relationship that meant bad luck to the soldiers of that day (this is a superstition similar to "13" in the West). During the Sekigahara battle the commander of the Western forces, Ishida Mitsunari, made his headquarters here after he had destroyed Fushimi Castle at Kyoto. Later the castle was given over to the Toda Clan, which held it until the end of the feudal period.

When the castle was at its prime it had five three-story and ten two-story turrets, as well as 26 watariyagura connecting various parts of the castle. In 1620 the donjon was altered. Burned in the 1945 air raids, it was rebuilt in 1959. Besides the donjon, there remain a moat and a few stone walls.

◈ Okazaki Castle

The original Okazaki Castle, built in 1452 (Fig. 33), is noted in history as the birthplace of Tokugawa Ieyasu. His grandfather became lord of the castle in 1524, and it was later given to Ieyasu. A three-story donjon was built within its walls about 1620, but during the Restoration the castle was dismantled except for the stone walls and moat. In 1959 a donjon was built on the castle site which reproduces the exact appearance of the original structure. In the basement of the present donjon is the foundation for the main pillars of the original keep. The castle site is now a public park which features, in addition to the reconstructed donjon, a well that is said to have provided water for Ieyasu's first bath.

◈ Inuyama Castle

Inuyama Castle is located some 20 miles north of Nagoya, perched high on a hill overlooking the Kiso River, giving a panoramic view of the surrounding country (Fig. 34). The site takes advantage of formidable natural surroundings for its defense. The fortification was first built in 1535, and its donjon was completed in 1537 —but at a different site.[2] It was originally the keep of Kanayama Castle located further up the Kiso River, but in 1599 it was dismantled and floated down river to its present site. This building is the only one on the castle grounds retaining its original form, and, as such, it is an excellent example of early castle architecture. It is a five-storied, three-eaved structure with tile roofs, white plastered exterior walls, and wooden walls on the interior, a contrast to the mud walls found in later castles. The design is basically three turrets placed one on another with hipped and gabled roofs. The donjon served both as an observation tower and as the residential quarters of its lord. The living quarters were on the first floor which is shaped like a trapezium. The top floor functions as an observation platform and is surrounded by a banistered corridor. The height of the donjon is over 100 feet.

Not merely an example of early architecture, Inuyama Castle also played a part in two military campaigns of some significance in history. The first of these was the Komaki Campaign of 1584, in which Hideyoshi and Ieyasu battled each other and Ikeda Nobuteru took Inuyama Castle for Hideyoshi. Ikeda had once been lord of the castle, so he was well acquainted with its defenses and had friends in the area. Although the garrison of troops was small, the castle was well protected by its natural surroundings of river and marsh. Ikeda, however, found some friends who helped ferry some of his troops across the Kiso and land them at a spot left unguarded by an accomplice inside the fort. The defenders, led by a Zen priest who had recently assumed leadership of the garrison after the commander's death, fought valiantly but were soon overwhelmed, and the castle became the possession of Ikeda and his son Terumasa.[3] Hideyoshi soon entered the castle, and he used it for his headquarters during the rest of the campaign.[4]

Sixteen years later, Inuyama Castle again played a part in history. It was one of the fortresses held by opponents of Ieyasu in his struggle for complete control of Japan. Along with the fortresses at Gifu and Takegahana, it bore the initial brunt of the struggle. After these strongholds fell, the opposing forces met at Sekigahara about 30 miles west of Inuyama.

In 1618 Inuyama Castle was given to Naruse, chief retainer of the lord of Owari Province. It is thought he added the top two floors of the donjon which altered the original form and design. The castle remained in the hands of the Naruse family until the Meiji Restoration, when almost all of the castle except the donjon was torn down. In 1895 the castle was returned to the Naruse family, who have retained ownership to the present. The castle has been designated a national treasure.

In 1961 the castle was hit by a typhoon and was somewhat damaged. A careful inspection disclosed that the elements, along with earthquakes, had taken their toll over the years, and the donjon was badly in need of repair. In January 1962 dismantling began, and it was discovered that the top two floors had been added sometime between 1619 and 1625. By September the workmen had reached the stone base and found that some of the stones had suffered damage during earthquakes, most notably, it is thought, the one in 1892. To be sure that the stones were sound, all of them were removed and inspected—a tremendous task since there were around 2,000, some weighing about 1,700 pounds. It was decided that about 200 were defective and had to be replaced. Stones were difficult to find, but many were eventually taken from the Kiso River. Time and lack of knowledge prevented replacing them exactly as they had been laid originally, so they were mortared together.

A 1:50-scale model of the donjon was made to guide the reconstruction, but work was delayed several times due to the lack of skilled workmen during various phases of rebuilding. As much of the original material as was salvageable was used in the reconstruction. When new materials were needed, they duplicated the original whenever possible. With financial aid from the Ministry of Education, the reconstructed donjon was completed in the spring of 1965 and was opened to the public.

◗ **Hamamatsu Castle**

Hamamatsu Castle was built by Ieyasu in 1570, and used by him as a residence, some say to get away from his ill-tempered wife whom he left behind at Okazaki. This change of headquarters was against the wishes of his ally Nobunaga because he felt it took Ieyasu from him and hindered their cooperation. The battle of Mikatagahara, fought a short distance from Hamamatsu, was an example of this cooperation. In October 1572, while Nobunaga was attempting to subdue the Buddhist monks at Osaka, Takeda Shingen of Kofu decided to attack him from the rear with some 20,000 troops. Their route took them near Hamamatsu, and Ieyasu was determined to stop them at Mikatagahara with a somewhat smaller force.[5] The defenders were routed after a sharp battle. That night Ieyasu left the castle gates open and ordered torches burned before the castle as a beacon to guide his scattered troops home. As Ieyasu had predicted, this maneuver confounded his attackers who dared not invade the castle for fear they might be drawn into some sort of trap. During the night a small force of Ieyasu's men attacked the enemy camp and raised havoc among them. Because of Ieyasu's stand at Mikatagahara and the threat of attack from the rear by another enemy, the Takeda forces withdrew, leaving Nobunaga unmolested.

During the campaign against the Hojo at Odawara in 1590, Hideyoshi, as previously noted, offered Ieyasu the eight provinces of Kanto in exchange for his holdings, including Hamamatsu. Following the siege of Odawara, Ieyasu handed over his old fief and moved to the new one with his headquarters at Edo. He regained his former holdings, however, after Sekigahara, and awarded Hamamatsu to a hereditary vassal of the Tokugawa shogunate whose family used it as a residence until the Restoration. During this later period the castle was torn down and the moats were filled in, leaving only the stone embankments. A three-story donjon was rebuilt in 1958 at the site of the inner citadel.

◆ Kanazawa Castle

The general area on which Kanazawa Castle is built was once the site of a small village called Yamazaki. A monastery belonging to militant Buddhist monks who were brought to submission by Nobunaga was also located there. In 1580 Lord Maeda started to build a castle that was completed in 1592. Under the Tokugawa regime, the Maeda fief of Kaga became the largest in all Japan, having a revenue of 1,000,000 koku. The castle was rated only after Edo and Osaka in magnificence (Fig. 35).

Because of its large fief, the Maeda Clan was kept under constant surveillance by the central government at Edo. Although the castle was formidable, the real center of military activity was at a temple called Myoryuji located across town from the castle.[6] Resembling one of the many temples in the area, the building is actually a seven-story castle under a roof that looks like a Buddhist temple's. Just inside the main door is a coin collection chest that is slightly different from those usually found in such temples, but not so different as to attract attention. Instead of collecting coins, the grate-covered box acted as an enemy collector, for it is in reality a trap door designed to send the foe on a death plunge. Inside the temple itself are secret doors and passages, and all windows on the interior of the building face the central well, which not only provided water but also featured a passageway to the main castle just above the water line (Fig. 36).

Along with his castle, Lord Maeda laid out a "pond garden" (now Kenroku park) that became one of the most famous in Japan. In addition to providing enjoyment for the lord, it served a practical purpose, for the water coursing through the streams also supplied the needs of the castle town. The streams terminated at a pond in the garden which was shaped like Lake Biwa near Kyoto, and the area surrounding the pond was made into a miniature of that lake.

The arts were not neglected by the Maedas. The Kaga-Hosho school of Noh plays was developed here. Famous Kutani pottery ware was first made under the patronage of the Lords of Kaga, who sent to China for ceramic experts to give technical advice. The samurai, who had little to do, began to practice the art of the tea ceremony, which in turn led to the founding of wrought iron tea kettles, another item for which the area is famous.

The castle of Kanazawa was no sooner completed than it began to suffer a long series of destructive fires. Beginning in 1602, when the donjon burned, there were some 30 fires recorded. After each, the damage was repaired, but during the Meiji era the buildings were torn down and in 1881 the second court was ravaged by fire. All that remains today is a turret, the Ishikawa Gate, and a 177-foot-long block structure. The gate was rebuilt in 1788 and was the main rear gate of the castle. It is divided in two sections that are at right angles to each other, forming two sides of a court. The other two sides are made up of turreted walls that are faced with lead tiles. The castle site is now the campus of Kanazawa University, and Kenroku park and the Lord of Kaga's mansion are open to the public.

◆ Himeji Castle

As the visitor travels across the Harima plain he notices a structure that dominates the whole area. At first it appears almost as a mirage, but as one approaches the city of Himeji one sees that the lofty white building is real. The traveler who alights from the train at this point and leaves the station by the front entrance is greeted with a beautiful sight—a 163-foot-wide boulevard leading to the White Heron Castle of Himeji. It is rated along with the castles of Nagoya and Kumamoto as the finest in all of Japan (Fig. 37). Since these two are only replicas of the originals, Himeji is now unrivaled as the masterpiece.[7]

The castle had its beginnings in 1346 when Akamatsu Sadanori built a fortification on the site while petty barons constantly feuded with each other and the Ashikaga shoguns in Kyoto. Himeji fell into the hands of the shogun, but it was recovered by the founding family in 1467. During Nobunaga's campaign to unify the country, he brought the Harima district under his jurisdiction about 1577 and gave control of this area to Hideyoshi who used the fortified site as his strategic headquarters. Between 1577 and 1580 he transformed the fort into a castle by building the triple keep and adding 30 turrets. Upon Nobunaga's death in 1582, Hideyoshi opened Himeji Castle to his comrades and, to prove his peaceful intent, distributed his stores of gold, silver, and rice, which had been kept there for use in case of war.

In 1601 Ikeda Terumasa was awarded the Himeji fief by Ieyasu, and, beginning in that year, started a nine-year building and expansion program on the castle. It has been estimated that some 50,000,000 man-days were expended under Terumasa's direction during the remodeling. The main donjon, built during this time, stands some 147 feet from base to ridge poll. The structure is reinforced by two timbers that run the full height of the building; these poles are over three feet square at the bottom. Other supporting posts are around the periphery and extend from the ground to the roof of the second story; they are more than a foot square and 38 feet long. The ground floor of this main keep measures 65 feet by 91 feet, and the succeeding floors taper until the fifth or top floor measures $29\frac{1}{2}$ feet by $42\frac{1}{4}$ feet.[8]

A principal problem in building the castle was the difficulty in finding enough stones. One of the walls of the main citadel even contained an ancient stone casket and lid, as well as stones from early pagodas. There is a legend that an old woman donated her seal, which was made of stone, and her sacrifice prompted others to renew their efforts to find enough stones to complete the castle sooner than expected.

According to another legend, a master carpenter by the name of Gembei designed the castle. After the palace was completed, an open house was held at which Gembei's wife commented that everything was magnificent but it was too bad the posts of the donjon slanted a bit to the southeast. Gembei was so chagrined that a mere woman could spot his failure that he climbed to the roof of the keep and leaped to his death.

Himeji is a typical example of the castle on mountain and plain. The top of Himeyama was leveled off and surrounded by high walls, and a river was diverted to fill the moats. Actually the castle is built on two hills that are separated by a small valley. The main citadel is on one peak, and the western citadel is on the other. The latter consists of a large court that is enclosed by a wall on two sides and a 650-foot-long tamon that starts at a turret on the southwest corner, runs north along the west side, and terminates in the northeast corner. At the termination point there is a turret arranged to be used as a residence.

Across the valley lies the main citadel, which is reached by going through several gates and turning many intricate corners. Along the route is the tallest wall in the castle, standing some 78 feet high. The main and three secondary keeps are within the inner compound. The secondary towers vary in height and number of floors. All four towers are connected with one another by bridge-towers; the arrangement of these connecting structures leaves a small inner court with the towers forming the corners. At one time a palace stood at the base of the massive main tower, but it was destroyed by fire. Near the southeast corner of the keep is a court called *harakiri-maru* which was used whenever it became necessary for a samurai to commit suicide. The area was also used to detain hostages.

The next lord of Himeji fief after Ikeda Terumasa was Honda Nakatsukasa, who married Ieyasu's granddaughter Senhime after the fall of Osaka Castle. It is said that the tower in the northeast corner of the western citadel was used by her as her bedroom. Because of this, the structure is referred to as *kesho-yagura* or boudoir tower. After Honda Nakatsukasa died, his son, Tadamasa, expanded the castle further. The Hondas continued as lords of the fief until 1639. Succeeding lords were Okudaira, Matsudaira, Sakakibara, Honda, and Sakai, who possessed the fief at the time of the Restoration.

Himeji, as already indicated, is the best-preserved castle in Japan. The outer court has been merged with the city, and a national highway runs on top of what was once the outer moat, but the main part of the castle remains about the same as it was in feudal days. Some repairs were made between 1910 and 1912, but they were not sufficient to check the deterioration that had taken place. Restoration work was started again in 1935, but the Pacific War interrupted the project. As fortune would have it, the castle escaped damage during the hostilities, and work was resumed in 1956 and completed in 1964 at a cost of nearly $1.5 million. The skill of 20,000 workers was used in this program. The base of the main keep was reinforced with concrete, and about one-third of the structure had to be dismantled and replaced. The castle is now a national treasure and is an excellent example of the Momoyama period of architecture.

◈ Hikone Castle

The site on which Hikone Castle stands was once the precinct of Sawayama Castle (Fig. 38). This castle belonged to Ishida Mitsunari, who, it will be remembered, was Ieyasu's chief antagonist and leader of the forces that opposed him at Sekigahara. Following that epic battle a force of some 15,000 men under the command of Ii Naomasa lay siege to the castle. After a day had gone by, it was agreed that the commander of the garrison, Ishida's brother, Masazumi, would commit suicide and the others would be freed. However, someone set fire to the donjon and all of Ishida's relatives took the lives of their wives and children (including Ishida's wife) as well as their own, and their bodies were consumed in the blazing keep.

Ii was given the fief by Ieyasu, and the name was changed to Hikone. As a means of weakening the resources of the tozama lords in the area, Ieyasu commanded them to help Ii to rebuild the castle and to strengthen it, a project that started in 1603 and took 20 years. The keep was brought from Otsu Castle at the base of Lake Biwa. This donjon, built in 1606, has three stories in addition to the basement in the stone foundation. Its architectural style is of the Momoyama period and is characteristic of Zen Buddhist structures. In some respects it is similar to the style found in residential designs of the era, of which the Golden and Silver Pavilions of Kyoto are examples. It is the only castle donjon styled in this manner. The site itself is on a hill overlooking Lake Biwa, and lake water was used to fill its moats. The castle also had a commanding position on the old Nakasendo highway. The city of Hikone still retains much the same layout as it did when it was a castle town. Its streets are staggered every few blocks so that the stroller can see only a short distance ahead.

The castle remained in the possession of the Ii family until the end of the feudal era. Its lords were among the chief counselors of the shogun, and Ii Naosuke was instrumental in opening Japan to foreign intercourse in the 1850's. For this, he was assassinated in 1860 outside the outer Sakurada Gate of Edo Castle.

Today the first and second rings of outworks have been reclaimed by the city, but the inner portion of the castle precinct remains much as it was in feudal days. Besides the donjon, there are the moat, stone walls, a gate, and three turrets still standing to give the visitor a good indication of what the castle was like in its days of glory.

◈ Sumpu Castle

The remains of Sumpu Castle are located in the present-day city of Shizuoka about 110 miles southwest of Tokyo. The city itself is sometimes referred to as Suruga in history because it was the capital of Suruga Province. It was important in the communications network, as the twentieth station on the Tokaido highway.

Sumpu was a Tokugawa town during the latter part of the 16th century, and it was here that, at the beginning of the Kanto Campaign, Ieyasu entertained Hideyoshi before they laid siege to Odawara Castle. Although Ieyasu lived in Sumpu before moving to Edo, he did not built a castle there until 1607, two years after he retired as shogun and returned to live in the town.[9] The castle was built as part of the old shogun's program of reducing the wealth of possible adversaries by requiring them to donate labor and material for castle building to benefit the Tokugawa Clan.[10]

During Ieyasu's retirement at Sumpu, many Westerners stopped to pay their respects to the ex-shogun. The best known of these was the aforementioned Will Adams, who really cannot be regarded as a visitor since he was a prisoner of Ieyasu. Among others, there were Sir John Saris of the British East India Company in 1613 and Don Rodrigo de Vivero y Velasco, Governor-General of the Philippines, who had been shipwrecked on the shores of Japan in 1609 (see Chapter 5). Descriptions of the castle by these visitors give us an idea of what it was like in those days. Don Rodrigo, who also left the vivid description of Edo Castle previously mentioned, tells how he was taken from his quarters in town to the castle in a palanquin carried by 30 men and escorted by 200 matchlockmen. Upon their arrival, an iron-bound gate was opened to them. Inside there were 200 more matchlockmen lined up, and about 500 paces further on they came to a moat and drawbridge. At this point he was turned over to another officer who commanded a second iron-bound gate to be opened. Inside this compound were 200 spearmen supported by more matchlockmen. After receiving respectful salutes, they reached the door of the palace. Vivero y Velasco also reports that Sumpu had a population of 100,000 compared to 150,000 at Edo, which, as we have seen, he had previously visited.

Sir John tells us of crossing some three drawbridges and going up a pair of large stone stairs before reaching the palace. He also speaks of "nightingale floors" that squeaked when trod upon and gave warning of one's approach.[11] As to the size of Suruga, Sir John reports that the population was every bit as great as London and its suburbs, which at this time numbered about 300,000.

Prior to the Restoration, the castle suffered many fires, and during the Meiji era the remaining buildings were gradually torn down. The castle was the home of the ex-shogun until 1897, and early in the 20th century the grounds were used to garrison troops. The site of Sumpu Castle is now a park holding all that remains of the once-grand fortification—the moats and some stone embankments.

◈ Nagoya Castle

Nagoya Castle was built by Ieyasu between 1610 and 1612 for his ninth son, Yoshinao. It was a magnificent structure befitting the status of Yoshinao, who was the first Lord of Owari Province and whose house was one of the three contingent houses of the Tokugawa family *(sanke)*. It was considered to be one of the three strongest fortifications of the country, although its strength was never tested by war (Fig. 39).

The Nagoya area had been the site of several fortifications dating back some two centuries before the present castle was built. The first to construct in the vicinity was Shiba Takatsune, who was a relative of the Ashikaga shoguns. The site he chose, as noted earlier, was at Kiyosu a few miles west of Nagoya. The Imagawa family is also said to have constructed a castle in the general area. Kiyosu Castle was held by the founding family until Nobunaga took possession of it during his struggle to unify the country.

The castle Ieyasu had built was on the site of a smaller fortification that was considerably enlarged for the new structure. He also had other motives for building a castle here besides providing his son with a base from which to rule his fief. For one thing, Nagoya was located in a strategic position on the Tokaido and would aid the shogunate in controlling the country. Hideyoshi's son, still in control of Osaka at that time, was, as noted before, a

Fig. 32. The four-storied keep of Ogaki Castle.

FIG. 33. The reconstructed donjon of Okazaki Castle.

FIG. 34. The donjon of Inuyama Castle.

FIG. 37. White Heron Castle of Himeji, the best-preserved castle in Japan.

FIG. 40. Entry to Hagi Castle. An observation tower was situated on the hill in the background.

FIG. 41. Detail of wall surrounding samurai homes in Hagi. The upper portion was plastered.

FIG. 42. An exact replica of the original donjon at Hiroshima Castle.

potential threat to Tokugawa control, and it was thought that a stronghold at Nagoya would help to neutralize that danger. Perhaps the primary reason for building such a magnificent structure was to weaken the financial strength of the tozama lords, for some 22 of them were prevailed upon to supply labor and material for its construction. Kato Kiyomasa, the master builder of castles in Japan, was the primary builder.[12] He was a crafty old gentleman who chose to keep the secrets of his skill to himself, so he used bamboo screens to conceal his activities when he built the steep stone base for the main tower of the castle. It is said that some 200,000 men worked on the castle, and that they completed their work "in a few weeks." Some of the building materials were brought from nearby Kiyosu Castle.

Precincts of the castle included the main court, second and third courts, and the western and fukai courts. Besides the main and secondary donjons, the main or inner court contained a palace used by the lord of the castle.[13] The residential quarters of the chief retainers were in the second court. The fortification of the main court was provided by high stone walls, moats on the north and west sides, and by a deep dry moat and high earthen walls on the south and east sides. The main donjon was six stories high with five sets of eaves. The roof of the first floor was covered with tile, but the roofs of the other floors were lined with copper. The first floor above the stone base measured 120 feet north to south and 105 feet east to west and had an area of 530 mats. The top floor measured 55 feet by 40 feet and commanded an excellent view of the surrounding terrain. The 157-foot-high donjon had an exterior of thick plastered walls that were painted white. The huge stone base was used as a storage area and also contained a well which, it is said, had gold thrown into it to improve the taste of the water. This main tower was connected with a two-story secondary tower by an earthen bridge. The ridge line was decorated with a pair of golden silver-eyed dolphins, eight feet eight inches high.[14]

During the feudal period Nagoya became one of Japan's two great castle towns (Kanazawa was the other). Because of its position on the Tokaido it was of immense commercial importance. It also became a center for the study of Confucianism under the patronage of Yoshinao, who brought in devoted scholars and built a hall for Confucian study.

The castle was retained by the Tokugawa family until the end of the Edo period. During the early Meiji period, when the castle was used by the Military Department as an army post, the troops reportedly defaced some of the art treasures. Later it was taken over by the Imperial Household Department, which preserved the castle and the palace as a historical monument and imperial detached palace. In 1930 the castle grounds and buildings were given to the municipality of Nagoya. On May 14, 1945, the old castle got its first and last taste of war, for on that date it was burned down during a fire raid on the city. Along with the donjon, the palace and its art treasures, other castle buildings, and the gold dolphins were destroyed. Fortunately some of the works of art had been removed before the raid and were preserved.

In 1957 a two-year-long construction of a reinforced concrete replica of the lost castle was begun at a cost of $1.67 million, plus another $120,000 to replace the dolphins. Made of copper, each of them is covered with 560 scales of 18-carat gold. The new donjon is used to display surviving art objects from the original castle and palace and also for other exhibits.

◀ Hagi Castle

Hagi Castle was built between 1604 and 1606 by the Mori Clan, lords of Choshu fief. Before the battle of Sekigahara, the Mori fief was the second largest in all Japan, but after that epic struggle, in which the Mori were on the losing side, their fief was reduced to about one-fourth its original size. Even with this reduction it was still one of the 10 largest in the country. The castle was laid out so that the five-story donjon was situated at the edge of the inner moat. It measured, on the ground floor, 65 feet east to west and 53½ feet north to south. The top floor was 20½ feet by 17½ feet, and the total height was about 47 feet. Fourteen generations of Moris lived in a mansion on the castle grounds, which were practically on an island, with a bay on one side and a river and moat on the others. An observation tower was placed on a hill behind the castle overlooking the sea (Fig. 40).

Choshu fief was a hotbed of anti-Tokugawa feeling after Sekigahara. Children were put to bed at night with their feet toward Edo as a form of insult to the shogunate, and they were told never to forget the defeat of their ancestors at Sekigahara. Dislike for the Tokugawas also may have stemmed from Tokugawa disrespect of the Imperial House; the Mori Clan claimed direct lineage to the imperial family and therefore had strong feelings of loyalty toward the emperor.

Hagi was the birthplace of Yoshida Shoin, the imperial patriot who advocated the overthrow of shogunate rule and a return of power to the emperor. At his school in Hagi he preached this philosophy until his death at the hands of the shogunate a few years before the Restoration took place. Many of Shoin's pupils became leaders of the Restoration era.

The leaders of Choshu were also resentful of the shogun's relations with foreign countries, and in 1863 their shore batteries fired on an American ship off the Choshu coast and effectively blocked the Shimonoseki Straits to foreign shipping. The following year a combined force of Dutch, American, British, and French warships put an end to the harassment, and Choshu agreed to pay an indemnity. After this incident the Choshu leaders came to friendly terms with the foreigners.

During the revolt against the shogunate, Choshu, along with most of the clans in western Japan, firmly supported the imperial cause. To show their complete loyalty to the emperor, the Choshu leaders were the first to tear down their castle (1874). The samurai were now without employment, but the head of the Mori Clan encouraged them to become peaceful farmers and raise fruit. This enterprise is still carried on today by their descendants.

Only the stone walls of the inner court and the inner moat of the castle remain. The base of the donjon can also be seen, and the huge stones used for pillar supports are still imbedded within the foundation. Steep stone steps running the entire length of several of the inner walls, overlooking the moat, provided a means of rapid troop deployment when immediate defense was imperative.

It is interesting to note that time has not touched Hagi as heavily as it has most other castle towns, and some descendants of samurai families still reside at their ancestral home sites behind old walls in the samurai quarters of the town (Fig. 41).

◀ Goryokaku Castle-Fort

This structure was unique in feudal Japan because it was designed along Western rather than Japanese lines. Built in 1855 by Takeda Hisaburo, a scholar of Dutch, it was laid out in the form of a pentagon and was designed to ward off intrusion by the Western world. Upon its completion it became the seat of the Hakodate magistracy.

During the revolt against the Tokugawa shogunate a group of Tokugawa supporters, led by Enomoto Takeaki, retreated to Hakodate, gained control of the surrounding area, and took command of the fort.[15] The rebels proceeded to form a republic with Enomoto inaugurated as its leader on December 28, 1868. The republic lasted until May 18 the following year when a siege conducted by imperial forces effected a surrender.

Not one of the buildings of this historic relic remains, but the walls and moat are still intact. Both the earthwork embankment and moat are over 95 feet wide, and the latter is used by the public for ice skating during the cold Hokkaido winter.

◀ Saga Castle

Saga Castle was built in 1613 as a residential castle by the Lord of Nabeshima. It suffered severe damage from fires several times during its history, notably in 1726 when the donjon and second court burned down, and in 1835 when the restored second court was again ravaged by flames. After the latter date the towers were not rebuilt.

Early in the Restoration Nabeshima Naomasa, who had been lord of the castle, was instrumental in encouraging able young men to take part in the new imperial government. These included Okuma Shigenobu and Soejima Taneomi.

Saga Castle was accorded historical significance in 1874 when a group of malcontented samurai rebelled against the government and captured the remains of the castle, which were being used to house prefectural offices. This group of former military men had agitated for an invasion of Korea to give them and their fellow samurai employment (the same argument brought on the Satsuma Rebellion). The rebel band was led by Eto Shimpei, one-time minister of justice, who opened the revolt on February 18, 1874. He had expected that all of Kyushu would follow him, but no one came to his aid. The rebels held the castle for 10 days before it was retaken by imperial troops, who captured and punished the leaders. This was the first revolt against the imperial government; the last ended just three years later when the Satsuma Rebellion was put down.

Only a gate, part of the moat, and some stone walls remain today.

◄ Hiroshima Castle

In 1589 Mori Terumoto began what would be an eight-year project: he built a castle on an island in the delta of the Ota River, calling this part of his domain "Hiroshima," which means "wide island." At the beginning of the 17th century, the Mori fief was given to the Asano Clan, who held the castle until 1871. During the Restoration all of the buildings were torn down except the keep.

The castle is noted for the fact that the Emperor Meiji resided there for seven months during the war with China (1894–95). When Japan became involved in the war of 1904–5 with Russia, the castle was used as a troop garrison.

At 8:15 on the morning of August 6, 1945, Hiroshima Castle, along with a large portion of the city, was completely demolished in the historic first atomic attack. Reconstruction of the castle donjon was begun in 1958. It is built on the original foundation and is an exact replica of the former keep in exterior appearance. The structure is five stories, 117 feet high, and is in the style of the early Momoyama period. The donjon houses a museum and a lookout (Fig. 42).

VII

Other Castles and Remains

◈ Akashi Castle[1]

Completed in 1620, this castle has turrets on each corner of the inner court and two turrets in the interior. The foundation for the donjon was laid, but the structure itself was never built. The castle site is now a park.

◈ Ako Castle

Most of this castle was torn down during the Meiji era, but a corner turret and the main gate have been restored. Near the latter is the site of the residence of Oishi Yoshio, who was the leader of the famous 47 ronin.[2]

◈ Bitchu-Matsuyama Castle

The donjon, a corner turret, and stone walls of this castle, built in 1683, still remain and are well preserved. It is a typical example of the castle-on-mountain type of defense, surrounded by densely wooden ridges and rocky cliffs. It is located in Takahashi City.

◈ Fukuchiyama Castle

Originally built in 1510, this castle was later enlarged into a magnificent structure. It had a four-story donjon and numerous turrets and turret gates in its several courts. Many of the gates have been removed and used at temples in the area, leaving only what is known as the Brass Gate and some stone walls on the castle site. A shrine stands where the donjon once was, and the castle grounds are now a park.

◆ Fukue Castle

This castle is also known as Ishida Castle. It was built in 1863 (late in the Tokugawa period) for coastal defense, but enjoyed only a short life as its buildings were torn down and the moat filled in early in the Meiji era. The gate and walls remain today.

◆ Fukui Castle

This castle's site had long been used as a defensive position known as *kita-no-sho*. The remains of the castle built in 1606 are still there today, including the stone wall of the inner court and the moat. During its time, it suffered from frequent fires, and in 1669 one great fire reduced nearly all of the buildings to ashes. The site has since been incorporated into the city.

◆ Fukuoka Castle

Built by Kuroda Josui and his son Nagamasa in 1607, Fukuoka Castle was known for its large size, numbering some 47 turrets but no donjon. During the Restoration the buildings were removed little by little until only the walls remained. The "tide-viewing" turret has been restored, and the castle precinct has become a park. Fukuoka Castle is also referred to as Hakata.

◆ Fukuyama Castle

Lord Mizuno built this castle between 1619 and 1622 on the order of Ieyasu. Some of the building materials came from Fushimi Castle when it was dismantled, probably including the existing tower which is said to have originated at Fushimi and is so named. The castle was auctioned off in 1873, and most of the buildings were torn down—all except the donjon, which could not be sold even for the nominal price of ¥20 or ¥30 ($10–$15) because of the expense of tearing the structure down. An air raid on August 8, 1945 accomplished the donjon's intended fate of 72 years earlier. A wooden gate with riveted iron bands on its face and the stone walls are still intact, and the donjon has been reconstructed.

◈ Funai Castle

This castle, in Oita City, was built in 1562 by Otomo Sorin, who had encouraged trade with the Portuguese and had a large part of Kyushu as his fief. The castle had a number of turrets and a three-story donjon, but all the buildings were destroyed by fire in 1743. The remains include part of the wall, a moat, and a turret built in later years.

◈ Gujo-Hachiman Castle

This castle, in Hachiman City, was built in 1559 and torn down in 1870 during the Meiji era program of castle demolishment. In 1933 the donjon, a corner turret, and a gate were constructed on the castle site. Wooden materials were used much in the same manner as in the original; these structures remain today.

◈ Hirosaki Castle

This was one of the most heavily fortified castles in Japan, surrounded by three sets of moats and covering an area of more than half-a-million square yards. Built in 1560 by Tsugaru Tamenobu (whose descendants held it until the Restoration) as a residential castle, it was the capital of Tsugaru district. (Some references give the date of construction as between 1601 and 1611). The original castle had a five-story keep that burned down in 1627 after it was struck by lightning. The site was then abandoned for 200 years. In 1810 a three-story turret was built in the inner court as a replacement for the keep, and this structure remains today along with much of the original castle precinct, including the western and northern enclosures, the first and second rings of earthworks, towers, and turret gates. The donjon is now a museum, while part of the grounds are used by Hirosaki University. The remainder of the castle grounds are now Oyo park, open to the public.

◆ Iga-Ueno Castle

Had the plans for this castle been carried out, it would have become a huge fortification. Instead, the donjon was blown down by a storm when only partially completed, and the plans laid out by Todo Takatora in 1612 were abandoned. The donjon that stands on the site today was built in 1935 and probably bears no resemblance to the original. Stone walls on the western and northern portions of the inner citadel still remain and are some of the highest in the country; a corner tower also survives.

◆ Kagoshima Castle

The castle town of Kagoshima was one of the centers of revolution in Japanese history. It was from here that Saigo Takamori led the Satsuma Rebellion (see Kumamoto Castle), waging his final battle on the hill where the castle once stood. During feudal days, 80 percent of the town's population belonged to the military class. As capital of Satsuma fief, Kagoshima was also the center of political activity from 1854 until 1868 when the leaders of this period agitated for and supported the return to imperial rule. In August 1863 the town was bombarded by the British in retaliation for the death of a British subject near Yokohama the year before. It seems that the Englishman got in the way of a procession of the Lord of Satsuma and was killed for his indiscretion. The castle itself was a modest structure with no donjon, built in 1613 by Shimazu, who was the lord of the area and whose descendants held the fief until the Restoration. Before the Meiji era the castle suffered from two great fires, followed by further damage during the Pacific War. Today all that remains are some stone walls of the inner court and sections of the moat. One part of the former castle grounds is now the site of a medical school, and another portion is a park. The stones used in wall construction are smaller than those found in many castles, but they are well cut for a nearly perfect fit; very few smaller stones are wedged between the larger ones to give proper alignment.

◈ Kakegawa Castle

Builders started to erect this castle in 1503, but it was not entirely completed until 1621. It was then that a three-story keep, which became the inner citadel, was built on the summit of the hill. The entire castle was all but destroyed in the great earthquake of 1854. The 19th-century residence of the lord remains today, and at one time served as the city hall for Kakegawa town. On an elevated portion of the castle site one finds a drum turret moved to Kakegawa from another location. The area once occupied by the castle is now a park.

◈ Kamegaoka Castle

This castle, located in Utsunomiya City, was encompassed by a quadruple set of moats and was one of the leading castles of the Kanto district. The buildings were demolished during the war which brought about the Meiji Restoration, and all that remains today is a part of the moats.

◈ Kameoka Castle

Constructed in 1707, this was the residential castle of Lord Matsuura. Of the original castle, all that still stands is the Badger turret, a gate, part of the walls, and some stone embankments. The grounds have been made into a park, and plans to reconstruct the castle were revealed in 1961. Located in the city of Hirado, this castle is also known as Hirado Castle.

◈ Kameyama Castle

Long used as a defensive position, this site had a fort on it as early as 1260. Sometime around 1590 a castle was constructed with a three-story keep and two sets of outworks. The buildings were torn down little by little during the Restoration, leaving only a turret-wall and part of a stone wall.

◈ Kashima Castle

This castle, which was built in 1807, had only corner turrets and no donjon. Most of the castle was demolished during a revolt in the early Meiji period. All that remains today are two gates, a stone wall, and part of the moat.

◈ Kawagoe Castle

Kawagoe Castle was built in 1457 by Ota Dokan, who is famous for constructing the original castle at Edo. Little of the castle remains today—just the Fuji turret, which was used as the donjon, and part of the moat.

◈ Kishiwada Castle

Construction of this castle took place between 1597 and 1640. During the Restoration, everything except the walls was torn down. A new donjon was built in 1954, but it does not resemble the original.

◈ Kochi Castle

The history of this castle can be traced to the middle part of the 14th century, but the castle did not reach formidable dimensions until Yamanouchi Kazutoyo acquired it in 1601. His enlarged castle was completed the next year and remained in his family until the end of the feudal period. The castle buildings were nearly all destroyed by fire in 1727, but the five-story donjon and a turret gate were rebuilt in 1748. More recently, the donjon was discovered to be on the verge of collapse because of severe termite damage. It was torn down, and reconstruction was completed in 1955. At its prime, the castle was thought to be impregnable because the stone walls were arranged to form zig-zag bends, with stone-dropping holes in the corners from which stones could be hurled and arrows shot at the enemy if he tried to climb the walls. The castle also featured fences with spears located between the walls and the inner portion of the castle, pointed in the direction of approach. Today the castle precinct is a park (Fig. 43).

◆ Kokura Castle

Started in 1602 by Hosokawa Tadaoki, this castle, with its five-story donjon standing on a 55-foot-high base, was completed in 1607. It was called the barbarian- or foreign-style castle because its design was unusual and because the advice of missionaries was sought in its planning. The donjon burned down in 1837, and other parts of the castle were destroyed by fire set by arsonists in 1866. The donjon was rebuilt after the Pacific War.

◆ Komoro Castle

Komoro Castle was completed by Takeda Shingen in 1543 and was surrounded by dry moats that were over 32 feet deep. Several gates, some stone walls, a storehouse, and the foundation of the donjon are all that remain today.

◆ Kubota Castle

The site of this castle, now in Akita City, had long been used for fortification. In 733 a fort was built here when the Ainu threatened the northern frontier. In 1603 Satake erected a castle on the location, which had neither stone walls nor donjon, but it was destroyed by fire in 1880. Efforts have been made to excavate the ancient fort.

◆ Maebashi Castle

Built in about 1590, this castle was later abandoned due to flooding of the Tone River. It was reconstructed in 1867, but was torn down a year later as part of the Meiji castle-destruction program. Today some earthworks and gun emplacements at strategic points are all that remain.

◈ Marugame Castle

This castle was first built in 1597, but reached its ultimate form only in 1644 when major alterations were made. It suffered greatly from fires in 1869 and 1870, which destroyed many of its buildings. The remains include the three-story donjon (which is visable from the Inland Sea), main gate, block buildings, and stone walls, which give an idea of how the inner citadel once looked. The donjon was repaired in 1950, and the castle grounds are now a park. The high stone walls around the inner court remind the visitor of those at Kumamoto and Matsuyama (Fig. 44).

◈ Maruoka Castle

Maruoka Castle was built in 1575 by Shibata Katsutoyo, whose descendants used it as a residence for much of the feudal period. The design of the three-story donjon differs from most castles, including, as it does, a banistered corridor just above the roof of the first story. It is a rare example of early castle construction. Another distinguishing feature is the castle's roof that is "tiled" with stones. At one time the castle was surrounded by a pentagonal moat that has since been filled in. All that remains today are the donjon and the stone walls of the inner citadel.

◈ Matsue Castle

Built between 1606 and 1611, Matsue Castle stands on Kameda Hill on the shores of Lake Shinji, whose waters fill the castle's moat. Built by Horio Yoshiharu, one of Ieyasu's supporters at Sekigahara, the castle remained in his family for three generations. In 1875 the fort was sold for ¥180 (about $90) to a demolitioner, but some local residents campaigned successfully to save the structure. Extensive repairs were made in 1950, and today the visitor can get a general idea of what the castle once looked like by viewing the five-story donjon, stone walls, and moat that remain (Fig. 45).

◈ Matsumae Castle

Built in 1606 by Matsumae Yoshihiro, this castle was burned

down in 1637 and rebuilt in 1639. In 1850 a new fortification, intended to help modernize the defenses of the country, was constructed on the site. This newer castle kept much of the old Japannese design, but the walls were strengthened to enable them to withstand artillery fire. During feudal times almost all trade for Hokkaido (then known as Yezo) passed through the town, and all travelers from Yezo to other parts of Japan had to obtain passports at Matsumae before continuing on their journeys. In 1875 the administrative building, three turrets, and an artillery position were torn down, leaving only the donjon and main gate. The former burned in 1949; the grounds are now a park.

◈ Matsumine Castle

This castle is somewhat rare because it was built in 1787, in the middle of the Tokugawa era rather than before or at the beginning of the period. Three years after its completion it was struck by lightning, and the main gate and other buildings were destroyed; the former was rebuilt in 1792. Little remains of this fortification today except a turret gate with a dolphin-shaped tile at the end of the ridge pole, now part of the local high school.

◈ Matsumoto Castle

First built in 1504, this castle was remodeled to its present form in 1597 by Ishikawa Kazumasa. It is a fine example of Momoyama-period castle construction and is beautifully situated on the Matsumoto plain with the Japanese alps as a background. The moats of the castle are of great depth. It has a six-story donjon, connected to the four-story southwest turret by a two-story tamon. In addition, there are the northeast and moon-viewing turrets. The upper parts of the buildings are covered with white plaster, and the lower portions are of wood that has been painted black, making the castle a rather striking structure.

◈ Matsuyama Castle

Completed in 1614 by Kato Yoshiaki, this stronghold stands on a

500-foot hill, affording the visitor a panoramic view of the surrounding area. The hill is densely wooden and has a ring of earthworks half way down the slope and another at the foot of the hill. In 1642 the donjon was remodeled from five-stories into a three-story structure by Lord Hisamatsu, who took possession of the castle in 1635. The donjon was destroyed by fire in 1844 and was later rebuilt. Meanwhile, the lord found that castle living was too inconvenient and built a mansion in town, permitting his chief retainers to do likewise. The castle survived the Meiji period as one of the few examples preserved as a specimen of the feudal times. During the Meiji period, however, some of the buildings burned down, and, in 1933, a lesser keep suffered a similar fate. Most of the inner court has now been restored, and the castle precinct is a public park. One can see the stones of the donjon foundation, which are hewed for a perfect fit with very few small rocks used as wedges. The outer walls of the inner court, typical of the castles build by the Katos (Yoshiaki's father built Kumamoto), are much higher than those found in most castle construction. These outer walls are of a rougher construction than those of the donjon base and appear to be cruder than those of other castles (Fig. 46).

◖ Mihara Castle

Mihara Castle was one of the coastal fortifications of Japan, built around two small islands with sea water filling the moats. It differed from many castles in that it had no keep. The main court was surrounded by rows of walls that had a total of 32 corner turrets and 14 gates. During the Meiji era the moat was filled in, and, in 1893, the walls were removed when a railroad bed was built through the area. Today the donjon foundation, part of a moat, and a corner turret are all that remain.

◖ Morioka Castle

The site of this castle has been used as a fortification for over 900 years, since Kiyowara Takenori was governor of northern Japan. In 1322 the Nambu family took possession of the area, retaining their sovereignty over it until the Meiji period. A castle was built on the site during the latter part of the 16th century, but the three-story keep and the inner and second courts were not erected until 1619. Except for the stone wall, the entire castle was torn down in 1874. A park now occupies the castle site.

◈ Nakamura Castle

Built in 1611 by the Lord of Soma, the castle is located on a hill in the Abukuma Mountains, now Soma City. The donjon burned down in 1670 after it was struck by lightning, and the rest of the castle buildings were demolished during the Restoration. The moat, main gate, and some stone walls and embankments remain today.

◈ Nihonmatsu Castle

Nihonmatsu Castle was founded in 1340, receiving major alterations about 1650. It was one of the fortresses that resisted the Meiji Restoration, and, as a result of a battle fought there, the castle was destroyed by imperial troops in 1868. The stone walls are all that remain.

◈ Oka Castle

This castle-on-hill type of castle, in Taketa City, was built prior to 1594. In that year, a three-story donjon and two turrets were added. The donjon was destroyed by an earthquake in 1769 but was later restored. In 1870 everything but the stone walls was torn down.

◈ Okayama Castle

The exact year of the founding of Okayama Castle is obscure, but it was built some time in the latter third of the 16th century. The donjon was destroyed at the end of the Pacific War and has since been rebuilt. It has six stories and five sets of eaves. The first floor is an irregular pentagon in shape, but the structure changes form

FIG. 43. The observation deck of this tower at Kochi Castle affords a fine panoramic view of Kochi City and the surrounding area.

FIG. 48. A corner tower of Takamatsu Castle. The high tide mark is visable on the moat wall.

162   CASTLES IN JAPAN

FIG. 49. Corner tower of Toyohashi Castle.

FIG. 50. The keep and tamon of Wakamatsu Castle.

as it rises until the top two floors become rectangular. Sometimes called the Crow Castle because it is painted black, the castle is bordered on one side by the Asahi River. The donjon is on ground gradually rising from the river, making it a castle-on-plain type. Besides the rebuilt donjon, there remain the moon-viewing and western turrets and some stone walls (Fig. 47).

◈ Osu Castle

Osu Castle was first built about 1331, consisting before the Restoration of a main donjon and a number of smaller ones. Most of the buildings were sold during the Meiji era, leaving today only four turrets. The castle site is now a park.

◈ Saeki Castle

This castle was built on the top of a hill and covered a large area. It had a three-story donjon, five turrets of three stories each, a one-story turret, four turret gates, and eight other gates, most of which were torn down during the Restoration. A gate, the donjon foundation, and stone walls remain today. The residential quarters of the daimyo at the foot of the hill also still stand, serving now as a public hall. Most of the castle grounds are a park.

◈ Sakura Castle

The moats and earthworks are all that remain of this castle, which was built in 1618. Before the Restoration it had a donjon of four stories and three sets of eaves.

◈ Sendai Castle

Sendai Castle was built in 1602 by Date Masamune, who fought on Ieyasu's side during Sekigahara. It was because of his assistance during this battle that Ieyasu awarded him the large fief of one of the vanquished enemies. Among the largest domains in Japan, it enjoyed a revenue of 620,000 koku and encompassed a sizable portion of northern Honshu. Masamune's castle had a large hall as his residential quarters, no donjon, and five corner turrets. Some of the buildings were torn down in 1871 and others were destroyed by fire in 1882, leaving only a gate and a turret, both of which were burned during World War II. The castle site is now a park containing stone walls and embankments and the moat.

◆ Shibata Castle

Shibata Castle was built about 1600 more to house troops than as a defensive installation. The general shape resembled a boat, inspiring the nickname *ukifune* or "floating ship" castle. The castle site is near the Kaji River so that, in case of imminent defeat, troops could retire to the stronghold and cut the dam, allowing the river to surround and isolate the castle. Only a gate, turret, stone walls, and part of the moat survived the Meiji era.

◆ Shimabara Castle

This castle, which was built in 1624, was at the center of Christian persecution that ended in the Shimabara Revolt in 1637. Although this rebellion has sometimes been proclaimed a religious war, it is generally agreed that it was a peasant uprising against oppression by the feudal lords. Many of the rebels were Christians, it is true, and after the rebellion was put down, open worship of the religion ceased. The walls and moats of the inner and secondary citadels remain, and the donjon has been rebuilt.

◆ Shinoyama Castle

Built in 1609, this castle had no donjon, but it did have very high walls. Its remains include stone parapets, moats, and stone embankments of the inner and outer outworks.

◆ Sonobe Castle

Sonobe Castle was a rather austere affair that had a three-story turret that served as the donjon; it was more a residential than a defensive castle. Built in 1619, it was torn down early in the Meiji era. The castle's precincts are now a park.

◈ Takada Castle

This castle was built in 1611 as a result of Ieyasu's program to reduce the wealth of the tozama lords. All of the buildings were demolished during the Restoration, and only the moat remains.

◈ Takamatsu Castle

Takamatsu Castle was erected in 1590 by Lord Ikoma, who was replaced after Sekigahara by a member of the Matsudaira family (kin of the Tokugawas). It is a rare coastal castle, and its moats are filled with sea water. The donjon was isolated by a moat and was connected with the rest of the castle by bridges. The stone walls retaining the donjon fill are of very crude stone work, the stones appearing to be just piled on one another with little or no fitting. The donjon was unique in construction—the lower two floors were built out over the foundation, and the upper two floors (it had four in all) protruded over the lower two. The castle's destruction came in 1884, leaving only two turrets, a gate, walls, and moat. The castle precinct, which is now a park, no longer borders the sea because the area on that side has been filled and reclaimed (Fig. 48).

◈ Takasaki Castle

Built in 1597, this castle had only earthworks and a moat for defense and no stone embankments. The castle buildings were destoyed in 1870, and only the moat and earthworks remain.

◈ Tanabe Castle

This castle, located in Maizuru City, was founded late in the 16th century. Although its natural surroundings did not add to its fortification (it was a plain-type castle), it was cleverly designed so that a relatively small force could defend it against large numbers. It is said that Hosokawa Yusai, with 500 men, held out against 15,000 men of Ishida's army during the battle of Sekigahara at Tanabe. It was abandoned during the Restoration. In 1940 a private citizen had a corner turret restored.

◈ Tatebayashi Castle

Built in 1530, Tatebayashi Castle was later abandoned, only to be rebuilt in 1708. Part of the moat and some earthworks remain.

◈ Tokushima Castle

This castle was built in 1586. All of the buildings were torn down in 1875, leaving only the Eagle Gate, which was burned during the Pacific War. The castle site is now a park, and only the stone walls and part of the moat remain.

◈ Tottori Castle

Tottori Castle was built in 1545 as a hill-type castle. The inner court had a three-story donjon and a turret, which, along with other castle buildings, were destroyed in 1879. The remains include the stone base of the donjon, an observation tower, and the first ring of outworks.

◈ Toyama Castle

This castle was built by Sassa Narimasa, one of Nobunaga's generals, in 1579. Fire destroyed it in 1609, and reconstruction was completed in 1640. The fief of Toyama later became part of the Maeda Clan holdings (they had their headquarters at Kanazawa). Over the years the castle lost much of its original appearance. A restoration program was undertaken after the Pacific War, but the reconstructed donjon and turret do not resemble the originals.

◈ Toyohashi Castle

Although this castle was built in 1505, it was altered and renovated off and on until the Meiji period. Held by the Matsudaira Clan, it was an important station on the old Tokaido highway. The buildings were torn down in 1870 when an army regiment was stationed there. At the end of World War II the castle grounds were made into a park, and a turret was reconstructed in 1954 (Fig. 49).

◈ Tsu Castle

Tsu Castle once boasted both a five-story and a smaller donjon which were completed in 1580. The fief was given to the Todo Clan in 1608, and they used it as a residential castle. During the Restoration the buildings were sold, leaving nothing but the stone walls and inner moat. A three-story corner turret was rebuilt in 1958. The castle grounds are now used for public buildings.

◈ Tsuchiura Castle

This castle was started in 1403 and was altered through the years. The only part that remains today is the Drum Turret Gate, which was remodeled in 1656. The castle was designed so it could be defended by allowing water from nearby Lake Kasumigaura to flood the area surrounding the castle and isolate it from the enemy. Most of the buildings were destroyed by fire in 1884; the castle site is now a park.

◈ Tsuyama Castle

Nothing remains of this castle, which was built in 1616. It had a five-story donjon similar to that of Kokura Castle in that the fourth and fifth floors were the same size and had no eaves between them. The castle was torn down during the Meiji period, leaving a site that is used as a park today.

◈ Ueda Castle

This castle was built in 1583 by Sanada Masayuki, who in 1614 and 1615 helped Hideyori defend Osaka Castle. In the inner court is a 65-foot-deep well that is said to contain an escapement. Repaired and remodeled in 1625, the buildings were sold to the public during the Meiji period with a turret going for around ¥6 (about $3) A corner turret was returned and restored after World War II, and it stands today along with two other turrets, the first ring of earthworks, and the stone walls of the inner court.

◈ Usuki Castle

Usuki Castle was built by Otomo Sorin in 1653. The site is now a park and contains the donjon foundation, a moat, stone walls, earthworks, and two turrets. The latter have undergone repairs over the years, and their original appearance has been altered.

◈ Uwajima Castle

Started in 1665 by Todo Takatora and completed in 1671 by Date Hidemune, this castle was shaped like an irregular pentagon. During the Restoration most of the castle was torn down, and only the donjon, main gate, and a few buildings were left standing. The main gate was burned during the Pacific War, leaving the donjon known for its rare design that includes a front porch. The castle area is now a park.

◈ Wakamatsu Castle

Also known as Tsurugajo, this castle was first built by Naomori Ashina in 1384. It was further developed about 1590, and the seven-story keep was later remodeled to a five-story structure. A major base of resistance against the overthrow of feudalism in 1868, the castle was torn down in 1876. In 1965 a reinforced concrete replica of the donjon was built along with the tamon and a gate, but the buildings—used as a museum—do not rest on the original foundations because of weight. Many of the original walls and the moat around the inner citadel remain, as do the foundations of several corner turrets and some old stone steps. Steps leading to the top of the wall by the main gate are of unusual design, running at right angles to the wall rather than parallel to it (see page 40). The castle is in Aizu-Wakamatsu City, and the precinct is now a park (Fig. 50).

◆ Wakayama Castle

This castle was built in 1585 by Hideyoshi after he had subdued Kii Province. He later turned it over to his relative Hidenaga. Ieyasu's tenth son, Yorinobu, became lord of the castle in 1619, and his descendants possessed it until Restoration days. This family was one of the three main branches of the Tokugawa family (along with those at Nagoya and Mito). The castle was altered in 1600 and was damaged by fire in 1813. After the donjon was destroyed by lightning in 1845, a new three-story donjon was built in 1850. Most of the castle buildings were torn down during the Restoration, leaving only the turret and a donjon which was destroyed during World War II but was rebuilt in 1958. The castle grounds are now a park containing the rebuilt donjon, a turret, and several gates.

◆ Yonago Castle

Built in 1602, this castle had a moat filled with sea water that made the castle a virtual island. The donjon was once the finest in the San-in district, but it was sold in 1874 for ¥30 (about $15) and used for firewood.

◆ Yonezawa Castle

A manor house that later was converted into a castle stood on this site by 1238, but it was not until 1601 that the Uesugi family established itself in the area and used the castle as a residence. A simple structure with no donjon, it was completely destroyed during the Restoration, leaving a site that is now used as a park and for public buildings.

Notes

(For source information, see Bibliography.)

CHAPTER I:

1. The *Kojiki* is the first recorded history of Japan. It consists of legends that had been handed down by word of mouth through generations and were finally recorded in the 7th century after the Japanese acquired a written language from China.

2. Garbutt, "Military Works in Old Japan."

3. The Soga Clan was a powerful court-noble family in 6th- and 7th-century Japan and, for all practical purposes, ruled the country. The Soga were the champions of Buddhism when it came to Japan in the 6th century.

4. The Ainu are a vanishing race of Caucasian stock who are found mostly on the island of Hokkaido. They are believed to have come to Japan from Siberia over 7,000 years ago, settling on Hokkaido and as far south on Honshu as the Kanto plain (the Tokyo area). The Japanese on the other hand are believed to have come from Asia via Korea and/or the Ryukyu Islands and to have first settled on the island of Kyushu.

5. Garbutt, p. 51.

6. Ruins of the wall may be seen today at Genkai Quasi National Park on Kyushu.

7. Europeans were vaguely aware of the existence of Japan as a result of Marco Polo's travels in China nearly three centuries earlier. Although he had not visited the island country, Marco Polo had heard of it from his Chinese hosts.

CHAPTER II:

1. Yoshiaki maintained the title but not the position of shogun until his death in 1597. The country was thus without a shogun from 1573 until Ieyasu was appointed to the position in 1603. Yoshiaki was a thorn in Nobunaga's

side even after he was deposed because he went from one of Nobunaga's enemies to another trying to get them to take up his cause.

2. See Chapter IV.

3. The same method of control was employed by the Tokugawa regime.

4. The taxes levied against the farmer usually left him with just enough for a subsistence level of living.

5. In Japan's middle ages there was a class of soldier-farmer who kept arms for his own defense and for use when called to battle by his lord. The result of these two reforms was to separate forever the two classes, a policy that was observed until the end of the feudal period.

6. It is thought that the Portuguese helped with the design of these two fortresses.

7. Lords related to the Tokugawa or those who were their hereditary vassals were called *fudai* lords. Although they had smaller holdings than the *tozama* (rarely over 50,000 koku as compared to up to 1,000,000 koku), they were more privileged.

8. Some well-known firms of today trace their beginnings to rather early in this period. The social scale of feudal Japan, from top to bottom, was warrior, farmer, artisan, merchant. At the very bottom were the Eta, who were classified as outcasts and did not count at all.

CHAPTER IV:

1. Rapid adoption is not meant to imply that every man in the various armies was armed with a musket. These weapons were in short supply for more than a century, but many armies had enough of them to necessitate a change in tactics and defense.

2. Some of the building materials used were taken from Nijo Palace (not to be confused with Nijo Castle), which Nobunaga had built for Shogun Ashikaga Yoshiaki.

3. Kyoto was thought to be a poor place for a military base because it was too vulnerable and sprawling to defend. It was also a hotspot for plots and intrigue, with conflict a constant and unavoidable threat.

4. According to Sansom in his *History of Japan*, vol. 2 (p. 301), the workmen were "encouraged by music" played by a small orchestra made up of townswomen.

5. The walls of Azuchi were rather crude compared to wall construction of later castles. The former consisted of stones laid one upon another against an earth embankment. Many of the later castle walls were better fitted into place, and corner blocks were hewed for a near-perfect fit.

6. By 1582 the population had reached about 5,000.

7. This policy was not unique with Azuchi, nor did it originate there, for it was used to some degree by most of the warlords of the time. Nobunaga, for instance, also followed the free-trade concept at Kano, his castle town at Gifu.

8. Akechi is said to have treated the missionaries well.

9. *History of Japan,* vol. 2, p. 308. Another version of the destruction of the donjon was given to the author by the priest of the temple at the foot of Azuchiyama. According to this story, Nobunaga's son destroyed the tower because he did not have enough troops to defend the castle against his father's assassin.

10. Although castle architecture is said to be one of the few forms of Japanese art that was relatively free of Chinese influence, Osaka Castle may have been modeled after a Chinese fortress of the Han Dynasty called *Kan-Yo-Kiu.* The main difference is that the Chinese version had no moat, while the Japanese did. See Summers, "Notes on Osaka."

11. There were some 30 feudal lords involved in building Osaka Castle.

12. Ieyasu considered Yodo the weak link in the Osaka defense, and therefore concentrated much of his effort on her.

13. These provinces now make up the lower portion of present-day Chiba Prefecture located on the Boso Peninsula across the bay from Edo.

14. Jesuit missionaries reported that Ieyasu's forces were between 260,000 and 270,000 men, which appears to be somewhat exaggerated. The same sources estimated the Osaka defenders to have had the strength of anywhere from 120,000 to 190,000 and the number of ronin to be as high as 150,000.

15. Some historians feel that Hideyori's failure to enter the battle saved the day for the Tokugawa forces.

16. Later Ieyasu became concerned about her safety and offered her hand in marriage to anyone who rescued her. She was finally wrapped in several mattresses, dropped from a tower, and retrieved by Lord Tsuwano. She was given in marriage to another man, and the rescuer eventually committed suicide.

17. The others were Edo and Kyoto.

18. Before the castle could be used for this purpose, however, an earthquake (in 1596) did extensive damage not only to this structure, but also to Kyoto and the castle at Osaka. Sources differ as to where the Chinese were received: Kirby states Fushimi was repaired and ready for the meeting 50 days after it was destroyed; Murdoch reports the Chinese were received at Osaka since one corner of the castle was earthquake-proof and undamaged although most of the stronghold had been destroyed.

19. Jurakudai was dismantled in 1595 after Hideyoshi obliged Hidetsugu to commit suicide when he was suspected of disloyalty to the house of Toyotomi.

20. The story of the battle of Fushimi is taken mostly from Sadler, *The Maker of Modern Japan,* and Murdoch.

21. Sadler and Murdoch differ considerably as to the motivation of the deserters. Murdoch suggests that they were bought off while Sadler says that the deed was done by one Koga no Goshi, who received word that his family had been captured by the enemy and was being held hostage under threat of death unless he would cooperate.

22. The battle of Fushimi Castle was a prelude to the celebrated and

decisive battle of Sekigahara which, along with that of Osaka, put the control of Japan firmly in the hands of the House of Tokugawa.

23. Several sources give the founding date as 1603; however, most agree that 1601 is correct.

CHAPTER V:

1. There appears to be some question as to the connection between Hojo Soun and the Hojo regents of the Kamakura government. One source (*Murry's Handbook*, p. 147) states that Hojo of Odawara was a younger branch of the regent family. Sansom, in his *History of Japan* (vol. 2, pp. 243–44), states that Soun's origin was obscure, but that it is thought that he was born in Ise. He later took up service with Imagawa of Suruga and was known as Ise Shinkuro. Around 1490 he changed his name to Hojo (of Taira origin) as a symbol of his goal to displace the Ashikaga shoguns—just as the Hojo had displaced the Minimoto shoguns—and thus bring back Taira rule to Japan.

2. Some authorities give the date of 1494, but most use 1495.

3. Ujinori was also in command of Nirayama Castle, the chief outpost of Odawara on the east.

4. This final demand was sent in December 1589 to Ieyasu, who in turn delivered it to Hojo.

5. Ieyasu also undertook the task of preparing the way for the invasion by building rest stops along the Tokaido for the troops, making sure castles were in good order, and storing supplies.

6. The story related above is from Murdoch. According to a version given in the *Kanagawa Community News* (vol. 7, no. 3, p. 7), the castle on Ishigakiyama was made of stone in the traditional manner. The occupants of the Odawara fortress watched as the castle on the hill above them was built stone-by-stone, and saw it completed in a mere eighty days. On the eighty-first day, the men in the newly completed castle began to lob cannon shells over the walls of Odawara Castle, soon forcing the Odawara defenders to give up. Although Hideyoshi tended to be extravagant in the way he did things, it is not likely that he would have gone to this extreme. Murdoch's version more than likely is closer to the truth.

7. According to Delmar Brown, each loophole of the castle was armed with three muskets and one cannon. Hideyoshi was said to have had several thousand guns with which to destroy the stronghold.

8. Nirayama and Oshi held out until Odawara fell.

9. Murdoch states that Ujimasa sent his sons to Ieyasu to arrange the surrender of the castle, while Sadler, in *The Maker of Modern Japan*, says that the sons negotiated without their father's knowledge or consent.

10. The heads of Ujimasa and Ujiteru were sent to Kyoto for public exposure. This treatment of the vanquished was common practice.

11. Sadler says that Ujinao died at age 29; popular Japanese stories say he was poisoned.

12. These were in 1614, 1632, 1703, 1707, 1782, and 1853. In the great earthquake of 1923 parts of the remaining walls were severely damaged and the nearby imperial villa was completely destroyed.

13. According to the pamphlet sold at the castle site, the dimensions of the original were: hon-maru, 132.7 meters east–west and 120 meters north–south; ni-no-maru, 654.5 sq. meters; san-no-maru, 1,754 meters e–w and 1,091 meters n–s. Its stone wall was 1,455 meters long, and total outer defenses some 4,364 meters in circumference. (One meter=3.28 feet; 1 sq. meter=1,196 sq. yards.)

14. Kyoto remained the imperial capital.

15. See McClatchie, "The Castle of Yedo," for a detailed description. The circumference of the castle given in this reference is probably grossly exaggerated (25 miles) because it was some 10 miles when the castle was at its greatest.

16. *Ibid.*, pp. 131–32.

17. This policy affected both the tozama and fudai lords. They were compelled to alternate their residence between Edo and their fiefs, and were obliged to leave their families in Edo when away from the city.

18. Gates destroyed as a result of the quake are as follows: Fukiage, Ote of the West Court, Ote, Sakashita, inner Sakurada, Hirakawa, and Sakurada.

19. The others were Owari with Nagoya as its castle town, and Kii with Wakayama as the center of government. It was from these two houses that the shogun was chosen if the main line was unable to provide an heir for the position.

20. Tadaoki's wife was a Christian convert with the name Dona Gracia. Even though Tadaoki aided and sympathized with the Christian cause in the face of the anti-Christian policy of the government, he still was regarded as loyal to the shogunate. For details of this relationship see "Hosokawa Tadaoki and the Jesuits, 1585–1645," *Japan Society of London*, vol. 32, pp. 79–119.

21. The result of the rebellion was the final blow to the samurai cause because the Imperial Army was largely made up of conscript troops who came from all walks of life. The victory of these men served to dispel the samurai image of unbeatable warriors. Nevertheless, it required all of the standby army and reserves of 40,000 men to put down the insurrection.

CHAPTER VI:

1. See Cooper, pp. 131–33.

2. Orui and Toba say the castle was first built in 1440, but all other sources state the founding date was 1535.

3. Ikeda Terumasa became a vassal of Ieyasu and was one of his supporters 16 years later during the battle at Sekigahara. He also is noted for the monumental expansion of Himeji Castle when he was its lord during the first decade of the 17th century.

4. The Komaki Campaign (also called the battle of Komakiyama) ended in a draw. Both sides withdrew after a few skirmishes.

5. Ieyasu's force included a contingent of Nobunaga's troops sent to aid in the battle.

6. The structure is sometimes called the "Trick Temple" because of the deceptive use to which it was put.

7. Nagoya Castle was destroyed during the Pacific War; Kumamoto Castle was virtually demolished during the Satsuma Rebellion early in the Meiji period.

8. Ikeda also increased the number of turrets to 50.

9. Ieyasu spent about one-third of his life in the Sumpu area. He was known to expound on the healthful environment and scenic beauty of the place.

10. Several other castles were built about this time, the most famous and costly being the shogun's headquarters at Edo.

11. These floors were built to give the lord of the castle warning of possible assassins. The palace at Nijo Castle in Kyoto gives the present-day visitor an example of this type of floor.

12. Kato is said to have acquired his knowledge of castle construction in Korea when he was with Hideyoshi on his campaigns there. He built some formidable structures with nearly impregnable high walls, an example of which was Kumamoto.

13. This palace was similar to the one found at Nijo in Kyoto.

14. According to legend, a robber by the name of Kakinoki tied himself to a kite and was able to fly over the castle and pluck a few of the golden scales off one of the dolphins. One of them was sent to the Vienna Exhibition in 1873 and was nearly lost when the ship returning it to Japan was wrecked off the Izu Peninsula. It was recovered with great difficulty six months later.

15. Enomoto was familiar with Western ways because in 1862 he had visited the Netherlands, where he studied naval science.

CHAPTER VII:

1. Unless otherwise noted, the castle and the city or town of location bear the same name.

2. In 1703, 47 ronin, or masterless samurai, avenged their master's death by killing his tormentor. In doing so they offended the shogunate and were forced to commit suicide. However, their loyalty to their former master made them heroes to the nation.

Glossary

bakufu: military government headed by the shogun

daimyo: feudal or manorial lord. Under the Tokugawa regime the term referred to those who had fiefs yielding a revenue of more than 10,000 koku.

fudai: hereditary vassals of the Tokugawa Clan

han: fiefs or domains, although sometimes used in reference to clans

hatamoto: direct vassals of the Tokugawa House who had the right of audience with the shogun. They had fiefs with assessed revenue of less than 10,000 koku that were administered by the bakufu.

ishiotoshi: stone-dropping chutes placed in the parapet and on castle buildings to aid in the defense of vulnerable areas

koku: a standard of measure equal to 5.12 bushels; the yield from farm production stated in terms of rice or its equivalent

maru: name given to castle courts or baileys. The main and innermost court is called the *hon-maru;* second and third courts the *ni-no-maru* and *san-no-maru.*

masugata: a type of gate often found at castles. It actually is made up of two gates separated by a courtlike area. Entry to a castle compound is made by first passing through a small gate and then turning at a right angle to pass through the main gate.

mon: gate. The main gate is called *ote-mon* while other gates were given various names

179

ronin: samurai who had become masterless due to some misfortune that had befallen their lord. They were usually unemployable and frequently became troublesome by disturbing the peace.

samurai: men of arms; retainers of the daimyo

sanke: the Three Houses; three collateral houses of the Tokugawa family. The provinces of Owari, Kii, and Mito were administered by them.

shogun: military ruler of Japan

tamon: a building on top of the castle wall used for storage and barracks

tatami: grass floor mats used as floor covering in Japanese homes. They are about three by six feet, and the size of a room is stated in terms of the number of mats it contains.

tenshu-kaku: the main tower or keep of a castle

tozama: outside lords; those who were not hereditary vassals of the Tokugawa family

uguisu-bari: a type of flooring used in the inner portions of the castle palace. When walked upon, it made a noise that announced the presence of intruders. It is sometimes called "nightingale" flooring, an approximation of the Japanese name.

watari yagura: the inner gate of the masugata with a tamon-like structure built above it. Watari yagura means a tower that bridges both sides, in this case bridging two walls.

Bibliography

BOOKS

Beasley, W. G. *The Modern History of Japan*. New York: Frederick A. Praeger, 1963.

Cooper, Michael, S. J. *They Came to Japan: An Anthology of European Reports on Japan, 1543–1640*. Berkeley: University of California Press, 1965.

Earl, David Magarey. *Emperor and Nation in Japan: Political Thinkers of the Tokugawa Period*. Seattle: University of Washington Press, 1964.

Fujii, Jintaro. *Outline of Japanese History in the Meiji Era*. Tokyo: Obunsha, 1958.

Ienaga, Saburo. *History of Japan*. Tokyo: Japan Travel Bureau, 1964.

James, David H. *The Rise and Fall of the Japanese Empire*. London: George Allen & Unwin, Ltd., 1951.

Japan: The Official Guide. Tokyo: Japan Travel Bureau, 1963.

Kirby, John B., Jr. *From Castle to Teahouse: Japanese Architecture of the Momoyama Period*. Rutland and Tokyo: Charles E. Tuttle Company, 1962.

Murdoch, James. *A History of Japan*. 3 vols. London: Kegan Paul, Trench, Trubner & Co., Ltd., 1925.

Murry, John. *A Handbook for Travelers in Japan*. London: 1913.

The New Official Guide: Japan. Tokyo: Japan Travel Bureau, Inc., 1966.

Orui, N. and M. Toba. *Castles in Japan*. Tourist Library no. 9. Tokyo: Board of Tourist Industry, Japanese Government Railways, 1935.

Sadler, A. L. *The Maker of Modern Japan: The Life of Tokugawa Ieyasu*. London: George Allen & Unwin, Ltd., 1937.

———. *A Short History of Japanese Architecture*. Rutland and Tokyo: Charles E. Tuttle Company, 1963.

Sansom, Sir George. *A History of Japan*. 3 vols. Palo Alto: Stanford University Press, 1963.

———. *Japan: A Short Cultural History*. New York: Appleton-Century-Crofts, Inc., 1962.

181

Sheldon, Charles David. *The Rise of the Merchant Class in Tokugawa Japan, 1600–1868.* Locust Valley: J. J. Augustin Inc., 1958.

PERIODICALS

(Abbreviations used in this section: *FEQ=Far Eastern Quarterly; JSL= Transactions and Proceedings of the Japan Society, London; TASJ= Transactions of the Asiatic Society of Japan; TIJ= This Is Japan.*)

Britton, D. Guyver. "Kanazawa: Water, Trees, and Lordly Grace," *TIJ*, 14 (1967), 244–49.

Brown, Delmer M. "The Impact of Firearms on Japanese Warfare, 1543–98," *FEQ*, 7, no. 3 (May 1948), 236–53.

"The Castle Boom," *TIJ*, 8 (1961), 109–11.

Dixon, W. G. "Some Scenes Between the Ancient and the Modern Capitals of Japan," *TASJ*, 6, part 3 (1878), 401–31.

Garbutt, Matthew. "Military Works in Old Japan," *JSL*, 7 (1907–9). 46–65.

Gould, Rowland. "Hagi: The Town That Time Forgot," *TIJ*, 14 (1967), 260–65.

"A Guide to Old Castles," *TIJ*, 8 (1961), 112–37.

Hall, John Whitney. "The Castle Town and Japan's Modern Urbanization," *FEQ*, 15, no. 1 (November 1955), 37–56.

Hattori, I. "Destructive Earthquakes in Japan," *TASJ*, 6, part 2 (1878), 249–75.

"Himeji's Seductive Fortress," *TIJ*, 12 (1965), 190.

Kimura, Ki. "When Hokkaido Was a Republic," *TIJ*, 9 (1962), 174–77.

McClatchie, Thomas R. H. "The Castle of Yedo," *TASJ*, 6, part 1 (1878), 119–50.

———. "The Feudal Mansions of Yedo," *TASJ*, 7, part 3 (1879), 157–86.

Sekino, Masaru. "The Castle and Japan," *TIJ*, 8 (1961), 97–101.

Summers, J. "Notes on Osaka," *TASJ*, 7, part 4 (1879), 388–408.

Takeyama, Michio. "Rebirth of the Castles," *TIJ*, 8 (1961), 106–7.

Tanabe, Yasushi. "White Heron Castle—Relic of the Golden Age," *TIJ*, 3 (1956), 137.

Temm, Peter. "Matsue: The Long Ago in the Here-and-Now," *TIJ*, 14 (1967), 252–57.

Index

183

DATE DUE

OCT 31 '94			
MAR 12			
GAYLORD			PRINTED IN U.S.A.

Fig. 1. Location of castles in Japan.

KEY:

      * *Partially extant castles, either original or reconstructed*
      ** *Remains of gate only*

* Akashi 55
* Ako 58
  Azuchi 43
* Bitchu-Matsuyama 62
* Edo 25
** Fukuchiyama 45
** Fukue 85
  Fukui 29
* Fukuoka 77
* Fukuyama 65
* Funai 81
* Fushimi 48
* Gifu 36
  Goryo Castle-Fort 2
* Gujo-Hachiman 35
  Hagi 68
* Hamamatsu 34
* Hikone 42
* Himeji 56
* Hirosaki 3
* Hiroshima 67
* Iga-Ueno 50
* Inuyama 38
  Kagoshima 88
* Kakegawa 33
  Kamegaoka 14
* Kameoka 78
** Kameyama 49
** Kanazawa 27
** Kashima 80

* Kawagoe 24
* Kishiwada 53
* Kochi 72
* Kokura 76
* Komoro 20
  Kubota 4
* Kumamoto 87
  Maebashi 21
* Marugame 70
* Maruoka 28
* Matsue 64
** Matsumae 1
  Matsumine 6
* Matsumoto 19
* Matsuyama 73
* Mihara 66
  Mito 15
  Morioka 5
* Nagoya 39
** Nakamura 12
  Nihonmatsu 11
* Nijo 47
  Nirayama 31
* Odawara 30
* Ogaki 37
  Oka 83
* Okayama 63
* Okazaki 40
* Osaka 52

  Osu 74
** Saeki 84
** Saga 79
  Sakura 26
  Sendai 7
* Shibata 9
* Shimabara 86
  Shinoyama 57
  Sonobe 46
  Sumpu 32
  Takada 13
* Takamatsu 69
  Takasaki 22
* Tanabe 44
  Tatebayashi 23
  Tokushima 71
  Tottori 59
* Toyama 17
* Toyohashi 41
* Tsu 51
  Tsuchiura 16
  Tsuyama 61
* Ueda 18
* Usuki 82
* Uwajima 75
* Wakamatsu 10
* Wakayama 54
  Yonago 60
  Yonezawa 8

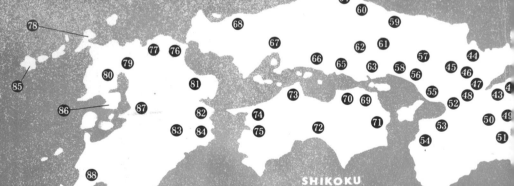

KYUSHU

SHIKOKU

PACIFI